Journey to Discipleship

By Cornelius Martin McKee

Dedication

To the one who saved me—Jesus Christ.

To my wife, my family, and every other person God used along the way.

And to every believer, new or seasoned, who wants to follow Jesus more fully.

This journey is for you. May you walk it with faith, courage, and joy.

Copyright © 2025 Cornelius Martin McKee

All rights reserved. No part of this book may be reproduced in any form without written permission from the author, except in the case of brief quotations embodied in critical articles or reviews.

All Scripture quotations are taken from the Holy Bible, New International Version® (NIV). Copyright © 1973, 1978, 1984, 2011 by Biblica, Inc.™ Used by permission. All rights reserved worldwide.

Cover design: Atika Ejaz

ISBN: **979-8-9938522-0-1**
Printed in the United States of America

Table of Contents

Introduction

Chapter 1: Author's Testimony

- Childhood Seeds of Faith
- Baptism at Age Eight—but Not Yet Ready
- Rebellion and Wandering
- First Marriage Ends and God Begins Stirring Again
- Second Marriage and Call to Ministry
- Tragedy and Loss in 2000
- Third Marriage and Baby in the Back Seat
- Fourth Marriage and a New Chapter
- COVID in the Philippines and Preaching Opportunities
- Transformation in 2024
- This Is Where the Journey to Discipleship Begins
- Reflection
- Prayer

Chapter 2: The Invitation

- Not by Works but by Grace through Faith
- Confession and Belief: The Heart of Salvation
- The Thief on the Cross: A Portrait of Grace
- Is God to Blame or Is It the Enemy?
- From Surrender to Transformation
- Cultural Christianity vs. True Surrender
- Crossing the Line: From Admirer to Follower
- Reflection
- Prayer of Surrender

Chapter 3: Growing in Faith

- The Battle between Flesh and Spirit
- Learning to Trust God Fully
- Building Spiritual Disciplines
- Scripture, Prayer, Worship, and Fellowship
- Progress Measured by Persistence, Not Perfection

- Growth Happens in Seasons
- Reflection
- Prayer

Chapter 4: A Growing Call to Serve

- Responding to the Small Yes
- Serving Like Jesus: The Heart of Our Call
- Sacred Roles, Unseen Service
- A Heart Prepared for More
- Service Is Presence with Christ
- You Are Not Alone in Your Service
- Reflection
- Prayer

Chapter 5: Called to Represent Christ

- Shining His Light in Everyday Life
- Representation Begins with Prayer
- The Power of a Life Well Lived
- Not a Title —a Daily Walk
- We Reflect His Character in Our Failures Too
- Serving in His Strength, Not Ours
- Ordinary People, Extraordinary God
- The Simple Invitations: Follow Me
- Reflection
- Prayer

Chapter 6: The Call to Follow Fully

- Jesus Modeled Surrender First
- The Wilderness Prepares the Worker
- Letting Go of Control
- Counting the Cost of Discipleship
- What It Means to Follow Fully
- The Lifeline of Prayer Is Surrender
- Reflection
- Prayer

Chapter 7: Becoming like the Master

- Christ Modeled Transformation Early
- You Were Made to Be Transformed
- What Transformation Looks Like
- Becoming like Jesus Means Serving like Him
- Pursuing the Lost like the Master
- Spiritual Disciplines that Shape Us
- Courageous Compassion: Truth and Love Together
- Becoming like Jesus Is Our Greatest Joy
- Reflection
- Prayer

Chapter 8: Walking in His Footsteps

- Aligning Your Life with His Example
- The Foundation of Scripture
- The Discipline of Prayer
- The Power of God's Presence
- Living Rooted and Built Up
- New Creation, New Walk
- The Mindset of the Master
- Walking in His Ways Today
- Transformation that Impacts Others
- Reflection
- Prayer

Chapter 9: Living as a Disciple

- Walking as Jesus Walked
- Remaining in Him
- The Fruit of a Disciple
- Love Is the Mark
- Letting Your Light Shine
- The Cost of Living as a Disciple
- Disciples in the World Today
- A Disciple's Influence
- A Disciple's Endurance
- A Disciple's Message
- Discipleship Multiplies

- A Disciple's Daily Decisions
- A Disciple Is Teachable
- A Disciple's Identity Is in Christ
- Reflection
- Prayer

Chapter 10: Making Disciples

- The Great Commission
- Empowered to Witness
- Every Believer Can Point to Jesus
- Modeling the Life of Christ
- Reproducing Reproducers
- Living like the First Disciples
- Paul and Timothy: A Model of Spiritual Reproduction
- Barnabas: The Encouraging Disciple-Maker
- Priscilla and Aquila: Teaching with Clarity and Grace
- Mary Magdalene: A Devoted Disciple
- What Their Lives Teach Us Today
- The Cost of Discipleship: Then and Now
- The Power of Generational Discipleship
- Disciple-Making in a Hostile or Distracted Culture
- A Final Call: You Are a Disciple-Maker
- Reflection
- Prayer

Chapter 11: The Spirit-Led Life

- Examples of Spirit-Led Obedience
- The Spirit's Power in the Early Church
- The Spirit's Leading in Everyday Life
- Crossing Boundaries by the Spirit
- Living a Spirit-Led Life Today
- Reflection
- Prayer

Chapter 12: Enduring in the Walk

- Do Not Grow Weary

- Joy in the Trials
- Run with Perseverance
- Pressing toward the Goal
- When You're Running on Empty
- The Discipline that Fuels Endurance
- Stephen: Enduring to the End
- Joseph: Faithful in the Waiting
- Keep Going
- Even Jesus Had to Endure
- Endurance in Gethsemane and the Cross
- Paul: Endurance Fueled by Calling
- Enduring When No One Sees
- Encouragement from Fellow Disciples
- Reflection
- Prayer
- Bonus Prayer for the Weary Disciple

Chapter 13: Perseverance

- Blessed Are the Steadfast
- Trouble Is Part of the Journey
- Perseverance Builds Character
- The Disciples after the Resurrection
- You Need to Persevere
- They Became Our Teachers
- Peter: From Denial to Devotion
- Persevering through the Silence
- Jesus Persevered for Us
- Be Joyful, Patient, and Faithful
- Paul: The Persevering Disciple
- Endurance in the Shadows
- Keep Going
- Reflection
- Prayer

Chapter 14: The Journey Continues

- Keep Walking
- You Haven't Arrived Yet
- The Road Is Narrow
- The Holy Spirit Leads the Journey

- There Are Seasons on the Path
- The Journey Shapes You
- Multiplying the Mission
- When the Journey Feels Hard
- Faithful in the Silence: John on Patmos
- The Finish Line Is Ahead
- Reflection
- Prayer

Chapter 15: Finishing Well

- Fighting the Good Fight
- Jesus—The Perfect Finisher
- Faithful to the End
- Redemption after Failure
- Leaving a Legacy
- Generational Discipleship
- Biblical Finishers
- Moses: Faithful in the Wilderness
- Caleb: Still Asking for Mountains
- Joshua: Leading Others to Finish
- Daniel: Finishing in the Shadows
- Simeon: A Life of Waiting
- Modern-Day Examples
- Eternal Glory
- The Master's Words
- Final Charge
- Reflection
- Prayer
- Final Blessing

Scripture Mention List

Full Scripture Index

Postscript: From My Heart to Yours

Acknowledgments and How to Grow Further

Introduction

You are holding a book that is more than just a message—it is a path, a path that begins with hearing the name of Jesus and leads to becoming like Him in every way.

Discipleship is not a church word. It's not a box to check. It's the invitation of a lifetime —and a daily walk.

I've walked this road. Sometimes faithfully. Often painfully. But always led by the one who calls, restores, teaches, and sends.

This book is for every believer—no matter where you're starting from. You may have just met Jesus, or you may have been walking with Him for decades. Whether you're barely hanging on or eager to grow more deeply, you belong on this path.

Each chapter is a step. Each step is a challenge. But every challenge leads you closer to Christ—and to the life He made you for.

You're invited not just to believe.

You're invited to become.

Let's walk this road together—all the way to the end.

Chapter 1

Author's Testimony

Childhood Seeds of Faith

I have always been a believer in Jesus Christ as far back as I can remember. I remember as a child walking into my father's bedroom, and he would be lying on the bed with his Bible in his hand. He read it every night. He told me that Jesus is everything and that we always need to remember him and love him throughout our entire lives. I can remember other times walking in and my dad would be there, his Bible lying on his chest, and he was sound asleep. My father really loved the Lord, and it was an amazing thing. I can remember that to this day.

Baptism at Age Eight—but Not Yet Ready

As I grew up, my father and mother faithfully got me out of bed every Sunday morning, loaded me into the car, and took me to church. I was involved in all kinds of church activities—Sunday school, junior church, and even Christian youth camp. At eight years of age, I thought I was giving myself to Jesus when I got baptized. But looking back, I realize that I didn't fully understand what that meant. I wasn't truly ready for that step, but I went through with it anyway. As the years passed, I continued believing in Jesus and attending church, but it wasn't until my teenage years that something began to change.

Rebellion and Wandering

In my teen years I drifted away from God. My parents eventually realized they couldn't force me to keep going to church or doing the things I was supposed to. They tried, but I rebelled and went my own way. It became a long, difficult road. Even then, I never completely forgot about God—I still thought about Him from time to time, but I didn't go to church, didn't pray, and didn't open a Bible.

First Marriage Ends and God Begins Stirring Again

That continued into my twenties, until around the age of 26. I had just come out of a divorce from my first wife and was living in Michigan with my new wife. That's when something shifted. We started attending a powerful church, a Church of God, and the way the pastor preached stirred something deep inside me. It brought me back to God in a way I hadn't experienced before. The pull was so strong that I felt a calling to become a minister.

Second Marriage and Call to Ministry

At the age of 29 I went to Spring Arbor University to become a minister. I was there for two years, studying the Bible and loving Jesus and God and doing all the things I thought I was supposed to do. One day I went to the church and said, "Hey—I've been in college now for a few years, and I'd like to work with the youth group," because I was studying to become a youth pastor at the time. The youth pastor said, "I don't need you and don't want you here." I took it as if God had rejected me. And so, I walked away from God for the second time and did my own thing.

Tragedy and Loss in 2000

Life continued until the year 2000, when things took a devastating turn. I was going through a difficult time with my second wife, and we had separated. One day at work I got word that there had been a serious accident out on the highway. I didn't know the details yet, but something in me was unsettled. When I got home the phone rang. It was the morgue. They were asking me to describe my wife and my son—any scars or identifying marks. That's when I learned the truth: they had both been killed in the car accident.

Please don't be sorry—because that was a change again for me. I prayed to the Lord to help me through it, to help me get by with what I had done, what had caused the separation. I just basically needed Him to help me. I know He had a plan for me someday in the future. I fell back on my college days when I was going to be a minister and never completed my studies.

Third Marriage and Baby in the Back Seat

A few years later I was at work and told my worker that I had forgotten to take money out of his check that he had borrowed for gas. There was a little baby in the back seat, and I knew it wasn't my worker's. His kids were teenagers. He said, "Oh, we're just babysitting him." And my worker asked his wife, "Do you have the $20 for the gas Mac gave me?" I looked at them jokingly and said, "Ah, just keep the twenty bucks. I'll just take the baby in the back seat." My worker looked up at me and said, "Are you kidding? The mom's talking about giving him up for adoption because she can't afford him." I said, "Sure—I'd take that baby in a heartbeat and raise him."

At the time I was going through problems with my third marriage as well. I was not living a Christian life—it looked as if I had always had problems with being married. But a few years after losing my wife and son in the car accident, I found myself caring for the five-month-old baby who had been in the back seat that day, a child whom I as a single father would later adopt and raise.

A few years later I went through another painful chapter. My third wife and I divorced after I discovered—through her own son—that she had been unfaithful throughout our entire marriage. The truth was hard to face. She hadn't married me out of love but rather for the money I had received after the tragic loss of my wife and son.

About a year later I was faced with yet another challenge. I had been dating a woman whose mother was diagnosed with cancer. She moved back home to care for her mom, and although we were already in the process of breaking up, things became more complicated. Her children had been living with us, and when she left, the plan was for them to stay with me so they could finish out school. A couple of weeks later, however, the two younger children went back to live with their mother—but the oldest one stayed with me. At that point in my life, I still believed in God but wasn't yet walking in full obedience to Him. My true transformation into a life of discipleship came years later.

The mom called around Thanksgiving and said, "I need my oldest child home because I need to have her take care of the younger ones while I'm caring for Mom." I said, "Okay. I'll bring her home for Thanksgiving and she can stay with you." When I went to the older girl and told her, "Hey—you've got to go home this weekend since your mom needs you to take care of your brother and sister," she said she wasn't going. "Mom said I could stay till the end of the school year and I'm staying," she said. I told her, "You can't do that. Why don't you want to go home?" There was an uncle who was handicapped and lived in the house with the mom. Then something inside me clicked and I said, "Did your uncle do something to you? Is that why you don't want to go back to that house?" She collapsed in my arms and we cried together. Her uncle had been molesting her since she was around six years old. That's why she didn't want to go home.

The church we were attending at the time was part of God's plan too. The county judge—the very one who oversaw family cases—also went to that church, and he knew the girl personally. On the Monday after the girl's conversation with me about her uncle, the judge called us into his office. After hearing what had happened, he placed her in my custody.

Her uncle was later convicted and sent to prison for what he had done. About a year after his conviction, we received a call informing us that he had been killed in prison—likely because of the nature of his crime. It was an incredibly traumatic time for both of us.

Through it all, her mother never showed up for a single court hearing to fight for custody. We returned to court several times, and each time she was absent. Eventually the judge looked at me and said, "Mr. McKee, will you take care of this girl until she turns eighteen?" She was only twelve at the time. Without hesitation I replied, "Yes, Your Honor. I love her just like she's my own daughter." The judge nodded, brought down his gavel, and said, "She's yours. You now have full custody."

Fourth Marriage and a New Chapter

A few years later my fourth wife came into my life. She's Filipino, from the Philippines. We were married January 3, 2014. She's very Catholic because the Philippines is a strongly Catholic country. We started our life together and we're still together today. However, we've had major issues, problems, and fights. And we got to the point at which we started attending church again.

In 2019 we were living in North Port, Florida, and had started attending a local church. Eventually we found our way to the one we now call home—Parrish United Methodist Church in Parrish, Florida. However, while we were showing up to church, our marriage was quietly falling apart. We were going through serious struggles and trials behind the scenes.

On the outside we looked like your typical churchgoing couple, but in reality we were just going through the motions. Yes, I read the Bible, but not with commitment or consistency. Deep down I knew I wasn't living out the calling I felt. I had always believed I was supposed to preach—but I wasn't doing it.

COVID-19 in the Philippines and Preaching Opportunities

I traveled to the Philippines a few times, but during the COVID-19 pandemic I ended up getting stuck there for eight months. While I was there, we attended a church and they asked me to preach—not just once but three times. I absolutely loved it. I remember thinking, *this is what I'm meant to do.*

But even then, I didn't fully step into it but now looking back, I can see that God was working on me the whole time. I could feel Him stirring something inside me—I just didn't fully understand what it was yet.

Transformation in 2024

In 2024 our marriage was full of fighting and pain. But then I viewed some videos from a group called "High Level Husband." That's when things changed.

The first thing we were taught in the group was to walk away from the flesh. And boy, I certainly had walked in the flesh all my life. I started watching *The Chosen* video series and reading the Bible again. I can't read much without falling asleep, like my dad, but I found an audio Bible online. Since February I've had the Bible read to me, and I'm now on my second full reading from Genesis to Revelation.

I've watched *The Chosen* series twice. I've also watched the movie *The 12 Apostles After Jesus*. The Lord has gripped me. He doesn't speak audibly, but He lets me know He's there. Once you start walking with Him, you change. The flesh is torn away. A new heart is put in you full of new desires.

This Is Where the Journey to Discipleship Begins

Now my order is in line. God the Father, Jesus the Son, and the Holy Spirit work on me every day. Do I still get down? Yes. But they lift me right back up.

My wife and I are getting better now. God is first. I had idolized my wife above God. I had idolized other things. I was doing things I shouldn't—pornography, masturbation, lust, and gluttony to name a few things.

I've given it all up now. It was so hard getting rid of the flesh. Through the High Level Husband group I learned that I don't need to depend on my old ways or on other people to fill what only God can. I love my wife, my family, and all my brothers and sisters in Christ, but my life and purpose now rest fully in Him.

Looking back over my life, I now see how God was always gently calling me, even when I wasn't ready to listen. The moments when I walked away revealed just how much I still needed to grow before surrendering fully. He still had a lot to teach me throughout my entire life, and that journey would take me through moments of failure, conviction, and ultimately total surrender.

Your journey may not look like mine. You might have grown up never knowing Jesus, or maybe you've walked faithfully with Him for years. Either way, we all start at the same place, in need of grace. This was the moment when belief began growing into discipleship and when following Jesus became more than just a name I claimed.

If you're reading this and thinking, *I've failed too much,* or *God couldn't want someone like me*, let my story remind you: He still calls. He still waits. And He still redeems.

This testimony isn't shared to highlight me—it's here to magnify the one who never gave up on me. Jesus is the true center of this story. And this is only the first page of what He can do in your life too.

Reflection

At the time I didn't realize it, but everything I chased—success, relationships, comfort, even distraction—was rooted in the flesh. I was running toward the world, not away from it. The desires of the flesh promise satisfaction but always leave us emptier than before. I wasn't just wandering; I was chasing things that could never fill me.

Yet even through all of that, God didn't give up on me. He allowed some of the brokenness I experienced to become the very soil where His mercy grew. What I thought was the end of my story was often just the place where He began something new. He used my wandering years to draw me back to Him, stronger than before. I believe now, more than ever, that "in all things God works for the good of those who love him" (Romans 8:28). Even the things I deeply regret have been redeemed by His grace.

Prayer

Father, thank you for never giving up on me—even when I gave up on you. Thank you for chasing me when I ran, for holding me when I fell, and for loving me in my weakness. For the person reading this, I pray you would show him or her that it's never too late to return, that his or her story, like mine, is not too messy for your mercy. In Jesus's name. Amen.

Chapter 2

The Invitation

Becoming a Christian is the first step on the path of discipleship, but it is not the same thing as becoming a believer. Before anyone can follow Jesus, he or she must first meet Him as Lord and Savior, understanding what it truly means to become a Christian.

Many people believe they are Christians because they grew up in church, were baptized as children, or identify with the faith of their family. Others think attending church, giving money, or trying to be a good person is what makes someone a Christian. But Scripture paints a different picture.

Not by Works but by Grace through Faith

Ephesians 2:8–9 tells us plainly: "It is by grace you have been saved, through faith—and this is not from yourselves, it is the gift of God—not by works, so that no one can boast."

So, becoming a Christian is a personal decision and not about receiving a gift or earning a title or a cultural identity. It is a moment of surrender, when you stop trusting in yourself and start trusting in Jesus. It's when you say, *Lord, I believe you. Save me. I want to follow you.* It is both the simplest and most profound decision a person can make.

Confession and Belief: The Heart of Salvation

Romans 10:9 says, "If you declare with your mouth, 'Jesus is Lord,' and believe in your heart that God raised him from the dead, you will be saved." Belief and confession—these are the biblical requirements. Not perfect behavior. Not religious heritage.

That is why this chapter matters, because many people assume they are Christians when they've never actually had that moment. They've never confessed with their mouths or believed in their hearts.

They've followed rules. They've followed religion. But not Jesus.

The Thief on the Cross: A Portrait of Grace

The thief on the cross (Luke 23:42–43) is one of the clearest examples. He never got baptized. He never attended a church service. He never went on a mission trip. He simply said, "Jesus, remember me when you come into your kingdom." And Jesus replied, "Truly I tell you, today you will be with me in paradise." That's grace. That's salvation.

Becoming a Christian is not about knowing all the answers. It's about trusting the one who does. It's not about fixing yourself. It's about being made new. As 2 Corinthians 5:17 says, "If anyone is in Christ, the new creation has come: The old has gone, the new is here!"

Is God to Blame or Is It the Enemy?

But there's something else that keeps many people from Christ—the belief that God is to blame for their pain, that God must not love them because of what happened in their lives. Maybe it was abuse, addiction, abandonment, or the death of a loved one. Maybe it was sickness, betrayal, or loss.

Here's the truth: God is not the author of evil—Satan is. From the Garden of Eden to today, Satan has been trying to destroy what God created as good. Jesus said in John 10:10, "The thief comes only to steal and kill and destroy; I have come that they may have life and have it to the full."

God doesn't cause evil, bring harm, or abandon anyone. Instead, He rescues, redeems, and restores. Therefore, when tragedy strikes, many people question God. *Why would He allow this? Why didn't He stop it?* But the truth is, we live in a fallen world, where free will exists and sin has poisoned the well. Even so, Jesus stepped in to redeem what was lost. His suffering on the cross wasn't a sign of cruelty—it was a sign of love.

Many people are mad at God for something Satan did. The enemy loves that. But Scripture tells us clearly in James 1:17, "Every good and perfect gift is from above, coming down from the Father of the heavenly lights, who does not change like shifting shadows."

From Surrender to Transformation

This is where surrender begins. Becoming a Christian is saying, "I no longer trust myself. I trust *you,* Jesus. I no longer blame you—because I believe in your love." That kind of surrender brings healing, because it opens your heart to the one who restores.

Hebrews 11:6 adds, "Without faith it is impossible to please God." That's what becoming a Christian is really about—not just believing God exists but also trusting that He is good; not just for others but also for you.

And for those who say, "I've done too much wrong to be a Christian," here's what Jesus says: "Come to me, all you who are weary and burdened, and I will give you rest" (Matthew 11:28).

If you've been carrying guilt or shame, this is your moment. Jesus isn't asking for your performance; He's inviting you into a relationship, and that relationship brings change from the inside out.

After someone becomes a Christian, the evidence begins showing, not because he or she is perfect but because God begins to work through him or her. Galatians 6:10 encourages, "As we have opportunity, let us do good to all people, especially to those who belong to the family of believers." Good works are not what save us, but they are what naturally flow from someone who has been saved.

You don't have to clean yourself up to come to Jesus. You come broken, and He makes you whole. You come lost, and He calls you found. That's what it means to become a Christian.

Let no one confuse this with simple church attendance or behavior.

Becoming a Christian is an act of the heart and a gift of God. It's where the journey begins.

If you've never made that decision, you can make it now. If you have, this is your reminder: never lose the wonder of what it means to be saved by grace through faith.

Becoming a Christian is not about simply checking a box, raising a hand in a service, or saying a quick prayer because someone told you to. It is about encountering the living Jesus Christ and choosing to surrender your life to Him. That moment may be loud or quiet, dramatic or simple, but it marks the beginning of transformation.

Cultural Christianity vs. True Surrender

One of the most common misunderstandings today is the idea that going to church makes you a Christian. Many believe they are Christians because they were raised in a Christian family or attended Sunday school. But Scripture makes it clear that faith is personal. It's not inherited; it's encountered.

When we say yes to Jesus, we're not just believing facts about Him—we're trusting Him with our whole lives. True faith involves repentance, a turning away from sin, and a new direction toward God. It's not perfection but rather a change of heart.

The journey doesn't stop there. Galatians 6:9–10 reminds us that even in the early days of faith, we are called to do good: "Let us not become weary in doing good, for at the proper time we will reap a harvest if we do not give up. Therefore, as we have opportunity, let us do good to all people." Becoming a Christian ignites something inside of us, a desire to love others as Christ loves us.

Some people blame God for the pain in their lives. When things go wrong, they don't always recognize the spiritual battle happening behind the scenes. They see only what's right in front of them—disappointment, frustration, hardship. But over time they come to understand that it isn't God who causes destruction; it's the enemy. The evil one comes to steal, kill, and destroy. But Jesus came to bring life. Maybe you've felt that way too. Maybe you've wondered, *Am I really a Christian? I go to church . . . but have I truly surrendered?"* The real question isn't *Do I go to church?* but *Have I given my heart to Jesus? Do I trust Him with my life?*

There are many sitting in church pews every Sunday who know the songs, the verses, even the traditions—but deep down they've never handed over control. They admire Jesus, but they don't follow Him. This is sometimes called *cultural Christianity,* which looks good on the outside, but there's no inner transformation.

Jesus didn't come to start a religion. He came to restore a relationship broken by sin. Becoming a Christian means entering into that restored relationship: fully forgiven, fully loved. As stated earlier, it's not about being perfect — it's about being made new.

Crossing the Line: From Admirer to Follower

This is the difference: the fans admire from afar. The follower picks up his or her cross daily. Jesus never said, "Admire me." He said, "Follow me." Becoming a Christian is about crossing that line—from liking the idea of Jesus to surrendering your life to Him.

Even the thief on the cross found salvation in his final hours. He had nothing to offer, no good deeds, no clean record, no chance to "earn" anything. And yet with a sincere heart he turned to Jesus and said, "Remember me when you come into your kingdom." And Jesus replied, "Truly I tell you, today you will be with me in paradise" (Luke 23:42–43). That's the power of grace.

So, let me ask you: Have you truly crossed that line? Have you gone from belief to surrender? From admiration to followership? Becoming a Christian is the most important decision you'll ever make. Don't leave this chapter behind without answering that question honestly.

There's a powerful simplicity in how Jesus meets us right where we are. He doesn't ask us to clean ourselves up first. He doesn't wait until we've got it all figured out. Becoming a Christian doesn't require a spiritual résumé. All it requires is an open heart. All He asks is that we come to Him.

Many people feel that they need to fix their lives before they can follow Jesus. But that's backward. We don't get cleaned up and then come to Him. We come to Him so *He* can clean us up. Grace always goes first. It's what opens the door.

Maybe you've been carrying shame—over things you've done, words you've said, or choices you wish you could undo. Jesus already knows. And He still says, "Come to me." When you become a Christian, that shame no longer defines you. You are forgiven. You are new.

Let me tell you this truth clearly: becoming a Christian is not about emotion but commitment. It's not about having a spiritual high. It's about handing over your life. That surrender may feel overwhelming at first, but it really is the beginning of genuine freedom.

Here's something you could reflect on: If you lost everything—your money, your health, your comfort—would Jesus still be enough for you? Becoming a Christian means He becomes your treasure, your anchor, and your hope no matter what life brings.

This journey is not just about securing a place in heaven. It's about walking with Jesus every single day—in your home, at your job, through your struggles, and in your victories. Becoming a Christian is the start of a relationship that changes everything.

Reflection

Becoming a Christian is not the end of the journey—it is the very beginning. The next chapters will help you walk forward in your faith with strength, clarity, and joy.

Prayer of Surrender

Jesus, I believe you are the Son of God. I believe you died for my sins and rose again. I confess that I have sinned and walked away from you. Today I turn back. I surrender my life to you. Be my Savior, my

Lord, and my Friend. Fill me with your Spirit and lead me forward. I receive your grace. In Jesus's name. Amen.

Chapter 3

Growing in Faith

After someone becomes a Christian, he or she often asks, "Now what?" That question is the start of a new journey, a walk of growth, trust, and transformation. Becoming a Christian is a moment of decision, but growing in faith is a lifelong process.

This chapter isn't about becoming a disciple just yet. It's about what happens in between—the time when we learn what it means to live for Jesus while still living in a world that tries pulling us back to the flesh.

Romans 12:2 says, "Do not conform to the pattern of this world, but be transformed by the renewing of your mind. Then you will be able to test and approve what God's will is—his good, pleasing and perfect will." In other words, *God's will isn't just a mystery—it's a plan for your life, and faith opens your eyes to it.* This is one of the first lessons for every believer: faith doesn't change just where you go when you die. It also changes how you think, how you live, and what you pursue.

The Battle between Flesh and Spirit

But the battle is real. Galatians 5:16–17 says, "Walk by the Spirit, and you will not gratify the desires of the flesh. For the flesh desires what is contrary to the Spirit, and the Spirit what is contrary to the flesh." That's where many Christians get discouraged. They thought salvation would mean instant victory, but growth takes time. The flesh fights back.

Walking by the Spirit doesn't mean you're perfect. It means you're learning to listen to God's voice more than your old nature. You're learning to lean on Him, not on your own understanding. As Proverbs 3:5–6 says, "Trust in the Lord with all your heart and lean not on your own understanding; in all your ways submit to him, and he will make your paths straight."

Learning to Trust God Fully

Spiritual growth begins with trust. Trust that God knows more than you do. Trust that His Word is true, even when the world says otherwise. Trust that He sees your tomorrow even when you feel stuck in your today.

It also means shifting your focus. Colossians 3:1–3 urges us, "Since, then, you have been raised with Christ, set your hearts on things above, where Christ is. . .. Set your minds on things above, not on earthly things. For you died, and your life is now hidden with Christ in God." Your life has a new direction now. You're not just surviving—you're becoming.

Building Spiritual Disciplines

The journey of spiritual growth doesn't happen at the same pace for everyone. For some it seems fast. For others it takes decades. I personally didn't begin walking fully in the Spirit until I was sixty-three years old. That doesn't mean I didn't believe before. It just took time for surrender to grow, for the flesh to be crucified, and for the Spirit to fully lead. Don't be discouraged if your pace feels slow. Growth is still growth.

The way we grow matters, and God has given us tools to help us: the spiritual disciplines. These aren't rules but are rather relational practices that deepen your connection with Christ.

Growing in faith doesn't happen all at once. It's a journey, not a lightning strike. Some days you feel strong while other days you wonder if you're making any progress at all. But the truth is—every step counts, even the shaky ones.

Proverbs 3:5–6 is not just poetic—it's practical. Trust is the foundation of faith. And learning to walk with God means trusting Him even when the road doesn't make sense.

Early in your Christian journey one of the most powerful things you can do is build spiritual disciplines. These are habits that feed your faith. The most essential ones are reading Scripture, prayer, worship, and surrounding yourself with other believers. When you do these things consistently, even imperfectly, your faith grows stronger.

Scripture is not just a book—it's the voice of God in written form. Second Timothy 3:16–17 tells us, "All Scripture is God-breathed and is useful for teaching, rebuking, correcting and training in righteousness, so that the servant of God may be thoroughly equipped for every good work." If you want to grow, you have to stay in the Word.

Prayer is your lifeline. It's not about saying fancy words; it's about being real with God. Just as a plant needs sunlight, your spirit needs prayer. The more time you spend with the Lord in conversation, the more you recognize His presence in your daily life.

Worship reminds you that God is God and you are not. It recenters your heart on Him, especially when life feels unstable. Worship can happen in church, in your vehicle, or in the quiet moments of your home. It's about placing Him above all things.

But growth also involves challenges. You will face doubts. You will stumble. Sometimes you may even feel distant from God. That's why community matters. Surrounding yourself with people who are also growing can make all the difference. Faith is personal, but it's never meant to be private.

Scripture, Prayer, Worship, and Fellowship

Reading the Bible is how we learn God's heart, His ways, and His promises. It renews our minds and strengthens our spirit.

Prayer is more than asking for things. It's about relationship. It's talking to God honestly and listening for His voice. Jesus prayed often, not out of duty but out of desire. If He needed it, so do we.

Worship isn't just music—it's surrender. It's fixing our eyes on God's worth instead of our worries. When we worship, we remember who He is and who we are in Him.

Fellowship is another key. God didn't design us to grow alone. When we surround ourselves with other believers—in church, in study, in life—we sharpen each other. We carry each other. We stay accountable.

And finally comes obedience. Growth happens when we don't just learn truth but also live it. James 1:22 says, "Do not merely listen to the word, and so deceive yourselves. Do what it says."

Progress Measured by Persistence, Not Perfection

Some days you'll feel strong. Other days you'll stumble. But God isn't measuring your progress by perfection. He's measuring it by your persistence. Philippians 1:6 says, "He who began a good work in you will carry it on to completion until the day of Christ Jesus." He started something in you, and He won't quit.

Faith isn't just believing in Jesus once. It's waking up each day and choosing to believe again, to trust again, to grow again. You won't always feel like it. The world will distract you. The enemy will accuse you. The flesh will resist. But growth comes when you keep walking anyway.

This stage, growing in faith, is essential. It's where you build spiritual muscle. It's where your roots go deep so your fruit can last. You're not becoming a disciple just yet, but God is preparing your heart. He's training your spirit. He's teaching you to recognize His voice.

Don't be afraid of failure — be afraid of quitting. Don't measure your growth by how you feel — measure it by how faithful you're becoming. And remember: God is more committed to your growth than you are. He is patient, merciful, and near.

So, keep going. Keep growing. Keep walking in the Spirit. You may still be in the world, but the world no longer owns you. You belong to Christ now. And that truth changes everything.

Growth Happens in Seasons

As your faith matures, so will the challenges. Growth does not happen in comfort. It is forged in adversity. The Bible never promises an easy path, but it does promise that God walks with you. James 1:2–3 tells us, "Consider it pure joy, my brothers and sisters, whenever you face trials of many kinds, because you know that the testing of your faith produces perseverance."

In seasons of difficulty, faith becomes a decision. When prayers go unanswered and the path feels uncertain, spiritual maturity means choosing to trust God anyway. It is in those moments that your roots grow deeper.

As with a tree, your growth happens in seasons. Some seasons bring visible fruit while others bring silence. But even in the quiet, your roots in Christ are expanding. You may not see the change right away, but God is still at work.

One of the most helpful ways to see your growth is to look back. Journal your prayers. Record your struggles. Write down what God is teaching you. Over time you will see just how far He has brought you.

And here is the encouragement: God is not rushing you. He is walking with you. Every stumble is a chance to lean on Him. Every small step forward brings joy to heaven.

As you keep walking, you may notice something else stirring, a quiet sense that your growth is not just for you, that God is preparing you for something more. And that is where the next part of your journey begins.

Reflection

Am I still trying to grow in my own strength, or am I leaning on the Spirit?

What spiritual discipline do I need to strengthen right now?

Where have I seen the most growth in my faith over the past year?

Prayer

Lord, I want to grow—not just in knowledge but also in relationship with you. Help me walk by your Spirit and not by my flesh. Teach me through your Word. Meet me in prayer. Help me worship in spirit and truth. Strengthen my heart to obey, even when it's hard. I trust you to finish what you started in me. In Jesus's name. Amen.

Chapter 4

A Growing Call to Serve

At some point in the life of a growing Christian, a new stirring begins, a quiet but unmistakable sense that God is calling him or her to do more. It's not a loud trumpet blast, nor is it always a clear voice. It's the quiet realization that faith is no longer just about you. It's about others too.

This is not yet full discipleship, but it is a doorway. It is what happens when spiritual roots start producing visible fruit. It begins as a nudge: *Volunteer at church, help in the community, Say yes to a small role, Speak up when someone asks about Jesus.* It may not feel big, but it's real. And it's the start of service.

Jesus said in Matthew 4:19, "Come, follow me . . . and I will send you out to fish for people." When He said that, He was speaking to fishermen: regular men, blue-collar workers. They weren't rabbis or scholars. They weren't looking for a calling. They were working, and Jesus interrupted them.

Responding to the Small Yes

The truth is, many of us don't go looking for the call—the call finds us. And at first it doesn't feel like a call to change the world. It feels like a chance to help set up chairs at church, to greet people at the door, to pray with someone in need. But when you respond to that first nudge, it begins growing.

Serving like Jesus: The Heart of Our Call

First John 2:3–4, 6 gives us the standard: "We know that we have come to know him if we keep his commands. Whoever says, 'I know him,' but does not do what he commands is a liar... Whoever claims to live in him must live as Jesus did." And what did Jesus do? He served, washed feet, fed people, taught the forgotten, touched the sick, and showed up.

A growing Christian begins realizing, *I want to serve because He served me.* That's why some people start by quietly serving behind the scenes, with no title, no spotlight, no recognition. But over time their faithfulness becomes evident. They pray with others, encourage the struggling, support their pastors, and offer help wherever it's needed. They don't seek leadership; their example leads others. What begins as a small yes often becomes something greater. That's how the call to serve grows.

This chapter is for the one who isn't ready to preach but feels ready to participate. It's for the believer who wants to say yes to God in the little things, because he or she knows that saying yes in the little things makes room for the larger things ahead.

Sacred Roles, Unseen Service

Not every calling is visible. Not every act of service is seen. Some of the most faithful believers are the ones who stack chairs, clean the building, pray for the pastor, bring food to the grieving, or make sure the lights are on Sunday morning. These roles are not small, they are sacred.

As you grow in faith, you will feel it: a desire to be used, a restlessness not for attention but for action. That's not your ego—that's the Spirit. He's preparing you, not for a title but for trust. If He can trust you with the *small,* He can trust you with *more.*

Joshua 24:15 declares, "As for me and my household, we will serve the Lord." That kind of service isn't always grand, but it's faithful. It's the daily, intentional choice to honor God in our homes, our jobs, our churches, and our communities.

A Heart Prepared for More

Sometimes the call to serve comes where we least expect it. You might find yourself ministering in a grocery store, on the job, or walking through your neighborhood. It could be a conversation at a gas station, a prayer offered in passing, or a helping hand during someone's moment of need. These are all unexpected ways we end up serving the Lord simply by being where He placed us at the right time.

Jesus affirmed this in Matthew 25:35, 40, when He said, "I was hungry and you gave me something to eat. . .. I was a stranger and you invited me in. . . . Truly I tell you, whatever you did for one of the least of these brothers and sisters of mine, you did for me." Small service in His name has eternal meaning.

You may not feel like a disciple yet. You may not even feel ready. But the desire to serve is evidence that the Spirit is at work. You are becoming faithful and are responding and following.

Don't worry about being perfect. Just be available. Don't wait to feel qualified. Just say yes.

The journey from belief to service is a beautiful thing. It's more than a sign of growth—t's a doorway into something deeper. You're not just learning more about Jesus; you're also beginning to live more like Him. As you grow in knowledge, you also grow in compassion. You are learning His heart, and His heart always leads us to love others.

So, if you feel that stirring, don't ignore it. That small yes might be the first step toward walking with Christ, a life shaped by love, service, and surrender. This kind of stirring is one of the clearest signs of spiritual growth. It's not just about volunteering; it's about stepping into God's call to be His hands and feet. Service is not something we do to impress God; it's something we do in response to His love for us.

Jesus didn't wait for His disciples to have it all together before inviting them to serve. He called fishermen, tax collectors, and other ordinary people to walk with Him. And through that walk He taught them to serve. In Matthew 25:35–40 Jesus makes it clear that when we serve others, feed the hungry, clothe the poor, and visit the sick, we are serving Him.

Service isn't reserved for church leaders, preachers, missionaries, or Bible teachers—*every* believer has been given gifts and opportunities to reflect Christ to the world around them. Whether it's greeting people at the church door, praying with someone in need, helping with meals, or simply offering a ride, it all matters.

Joshua 24:15 also offers a strong declaration that isn't just about worship. It's also about action. It's a commitment to live in a way that brings God's love to others. Serving doesn't always look big or public. Sometimes it's quiet, behind the scenes, and deeply impactful.

One day you might feel a tug on your heart, a desire to do something more, maybe to help with youth ministry, lead a Bible study, or organize meals for those in need. That's not random. That's God calling you deeper. This growing call to serve is part of His plan to shape you into the likeness of Christ.

In Matthew 20:26-28 Jesus reminds us that He came not to be served but to serve and to give His life as a ransom for many. If the Son of God came as a servant, how much more should we embrace that calling in our own walk of faith?

And it's not just what you do, it's how you do it. Service without love is noise. But when you serve with the heart of Christ, even the smallest gesture becomes eternal. Galatians 6:10 says, "As we have opportunity, let us do good to all people, especially to those who belong to the family of believers."

Sometimes we overthink what it means to serve, imagining it requires a big stage, a formal title, or years of training. Yet service often begins with simple acts of love. Jesus washed His disciples' feet and sat with the outcasts. He wept with the grieving. Our call to serve begins the same way, by showing up for people with love in our hearts.

One of the simplest but most overlooked ways to do that is by listening. When someone is hurting, your presence, your quiet attention—can be a powerful act of service. In a world filled with noise and distraction, being fully present is rare and sacred.

That is why there is no such thing as "insignificant" service in the kingdom of God. In fact, 1 Peter 4:10 reminds us, "Each of you should use whatever gift you have received to serve others, as faithful stewards of God's grace in its various forms." Your gift might be hospitality, encouragement, teaching, craftsmanship, or just having a heart that sees people in need.

And sometimes the act of serving grows us as much as it helps someone else. It humbles us. It reminds us that life isn't just about what we gain but also about what we give. God often works through our obedience to build our character.

If you ever feel unqualified to serve, remember this: Jesus doesn't call the equipped, He equips the called. Moses doubted his voice, David was overlooked, and Peter denied Jesus three times—yet God used them powerfully. He can use you too.

Ask yourself today, what is one small act of service I can do this week? Who around me might need a helping hand, a word of encouragement, or a moment of my time? Ask God to open your eyes. The opportunities are everywhere.

Service Is Presence with Christ

In John 12:26 Jesus says, "Whoever serves me must follow me; and where I am, my servant also will be. My Father will honor the one who serves me." This verse powerfully links two essential aspects of discipleship: service and presence.

Jesus isn't calling us simply to do acts of service—He's calling us also to walk with Him while we serve. It's not service apart from Christ but rather service alongside Him. Wherever Jesus goes, that's where His servant should be. That means we need to be near to Him, not just in what we do but also in who we are becoming.

This verse also carries a promise: "My Father will honor the one who serves me." What an incredible encouragement! God Himself notices our obedience, even the acts no one else sees. Heaven pays attention. Our labor in the Lord is never in vain.

You Are Not Alone in Your Service

So, when you're serving, even in the smallest ways, remember this: You are not alone. Jesus is with you. He is working through you. And the Father is honoring what you're doing in His name. That truth should breathe life into every step you take as a servant of Christ.

Reflection
- In what small way could I say yes to God this week?
- Am I willing to serve without recognition, just as Jesus did?
- Where might God be inviting me to serve, even in unexpected places?
- Have I been waiting to feel "qualified" before saying yes?

Prayer
Lord, thank you for calling me to more. I may not feel ready, but I want to be faithful. Show me where I can serve: in the church, in my neighborhood, at work, or even in silence. Help me say yes in the small things and prepare me for what's ahead. Give me a heart that's willing, hands that are open, and eyes that see the needs around me. I don't want to just be a believer. I also want to be available. Help me follow the example of Jesus, who came not to be served but to serve. In His name I pray. Amen.

Chapter 5

Called to Represent Christ

Once a believer begins serving and walking in faith, something deeper begins taking root: a realization that he or she is not only following Jesus privately but is also representing Him publicly. It's not just about what you do for God but also who you are becoming in Him. The way you live now speaks loudly to the world around you.

The Bible says in 2 Corinthians 5:20, "We are therefore Christ's ambassadors, as though God were making his appeal through us." This is no small assignment. It means your life becomes a reflection of Jesus—your words, your actions, your patience, your kindness. You are carrying the name of Christ wherever you go.

Representing Jesus is not just for pastors or missionaries. It's the calling of every believer. Whether you work in an office, stay at home with your kids, flip burgers, manage a team, or greet at the church door, you carry His image. You are the closest glimpse of Jesus some people will ever see.

Shining His Light in Everyday Life

This is why Jesus said in Matthew 5:16, "Let your light shine before others, that they may see your good deeds and glorify your Father in heaven." When your light shines, others see not just your actions but also the one who inspires them.

This call to represent Christ extends beyond Sunday mornings. It touches every part of life: how you treat your spouse, how you handle stress, how you respond to conflict, how you talk to strangers, how you love your enemies. Your lifestyle is your witness.

Representation Begins with Prayer

But representing Christ doesn't come from trying harder—it comes from going deeper. It begins with prayer.

Before Jesus ever preached a sermon, performed a miracle, or called His first disciple, He was led by the Spirit into the wilderness for forty days—alone, fasting, praying. In Matthew 4 and Luke 4 we read that Satan came to tempt Him not once but three times. Each time Jesus resisted by quoting Scripture.

His time of testing wasn't wasted—it was preparation for the mission ahead. Jesus didn't begin His public ministry until He had spent time alone in private preparation. If the Son of God needed prayer and time with the Father to prepare to represent heaven, how much more do we?

Prayer is where we align our heart with God's. It's where our motives are purified, our fears are quieted, and our courage is renewed. Without prayer we start representing ourselves, our pride, our wounds, our opinions. But with prayer we represent Christ, His humility, His grace, His power.

The Power of a Life Well Lived

Let's be honest: The world is watching. And it's not watching for perfection—it's watching for authenticity. When you represent Jesus, people want to see if you live what you say. That doesn't mean being flawless. It means being honest. It means repenting when you fail. It means forgiving when it hurts. It means standing for truth without losing compassion.

Consider a Christian business-owner named Sheila. She runs a small bakery, and everything about her shop is an opportunity to represent Christ. Her prices are fair, her staff is treated with dignity, her customers feel welcome. But the true representation comes behind the scenes: praying with a hurting employee, donating unsold goods to shelters, responding with grace when someone is rude. Her bakery isn't just a business—it's a platform for the gospel.

You don't need a pulpit to preach. Sometimes the most powerful sermon is the life you live under pressure. When people see peace in your chaos, kindness in your conflict, and hope in your suffering, they are drawn to the source.

This is why representation without prayer becomes religion. It turns into performance. But representation *with* prayer becomes revelation. It reveals Christ through our lives.

Matthew 5:16 reminds us that our good works aren't for applause—they're for the glory of God. When people see your life and glorify God, you're doing it right. That's representation.

Here's the hard truth: When we misrepresent Jesus, it can drive people away. Hypocrisy, harshness, pride, and judgment do not reflect Christ. That's why we must continually return to prayer. Ask the Spirit: Am I showing Jesus or just showing off? Am I helping people see Him or just see me?

This chapter is a turning point. You've gone from receiving grace to displaying it. You've gone from serving quietly to shining boldly. You are a representative now, not just of a belief system but of a living Savior.

Not a Title — a Daily Walk

Being called to represent Christ is more than a title—it's an identity. When we say yes to Jesus, we step into a new role. We are no longer just living for ourselves; we become ambassadors of the kingdom of God (2 Corinthians 5:20).

This means people are watching. Whether you're at work, with your family, or walking through a grocery store, the way you speak, act, and respond paints a picture of Jesus to the world. It's a responsibility but also an incredible privilege.

First John 2:3–6 says, "We know that we have come to know him if we keep his commands. Whoever says, 'I know him,' but does not do what he commands is a liar, and the truth is not in that person. But if anyone obeys his word, love for God is truly made complete in them. This is how we know we are in him: Whoever claims to live in him must live as Jesus did." These are strong words and a clear call to integrity. Representing Christ means reflecting His character in everything.

Our calling is to reflect Jesus nor simply in our morality but also in our relationships, our mercy, our courage, and our truth-telling. We're not just showing the world that we believe in Him—we're also showing them what He's like.

In Philippians 2:15 Paul writes that we are to "shine . . . like stars in the sky" in a crooked generation. That imagery is powerful. We don't need to be perfect to shine—we just need to be filled with His light.

You may not always feel worthy of representing Christ. But remember: God doesn't ask for perfection—He asks for surrender. Your humility, your honesty, and your obedience speak volumes more than a flawless exterior.

We Reflect His Character in Our Failures Too

There will be times when you fail, times when your actions don't reflect Jesus well. But God's grace doesn't quit. Every time you fall short is a chance to model repentance and restoration. That's also part of representing Christ, showing what grace looks like in real life.

And don't underestimate the power of small things: a gentle response, a prayer for a friend, a note of encouragement, a refusal to gossip. These are daily moments when Christ can be made visible through you. These small acts aren't done in your own strength—they are empowered by the Spirit of God working through you.

Serving in His Strength, Not Ours

One way we grow as representatives of Christ is by understanding that we do not do this in our own power but through His Spirit. Acts 1:8 promises, "You will receive power when the Holy Spirit comes upon you; and you will be my witnesses in Jerusalem, and in all Judea and Samaria, and to the ends of the earth." This is not a heavy burden we carry ourselves; instead, we become a pipeline for His power, His peace, His patience, His kindness, His goodness, His faithfulness, His gentleness, and His self-control (Galatians 5:22–23).

Every interaction we have is a potential opportunity to reflect Him. Whether we are at the grocery store, at the gym, at a restaurant, or simply within our own families, we can manifest His character and His compassion. This kind of representation cannot be manufactured or forced—it flows naturally from a heart that is full of Him.

Some people say, "Don't talk about your faith—just show it," but Scripture makes it clear that we are to do both (Romans 10:14–15). We must be ready to speak when the opportunity arises, but we must first make sure our lives reflect the transformation we claim to have undergone.

We must remember that we are not called to be perfect, we are called to be faithful. First John 1:9 promises us, "If we confess our sins, he is faithful and just and will forgive us our sins and purify us from all unrighteousness," freeing us to serve without shame or guilt.

When we serve with pure motives, not for recognition or earthly rewards, we become a powerful testimony to the world (Colossians 3:23–24). We do everything as unto the Lord, trusting Him to produce eternal fruit from our efforts.

Last, remember that you do not serve alone. The body of Christ is meant to work together (1 Corinthians 12), each person employing his or her respective gifts in unity, strengthening and honoring one another as we collectively reflect Him.

Consider the apostle Paul, whose transformation from persecutor to preacher shows us that God can redeem anyone (Acts 9). His testimony stands as a powerful reminder that our past doesn't disqualify us; instead, it prepares us for greater service. Paul wrote in 1 Timothy 1:15–16, "Here is a trustworthy saying that deserves full acceptance: Christ Jesus came into the world to save sinners—of whom I am the worst. But for that very reason I was shown mercy, so that in me, the worst of sinners, Christ Jesus might demonstrate his immense patience as an example for those who would believe in him and receive eternal life."

This kind of transformation should produce humility and compassion within us, fueling our service toward others instead of fostering a judgmental spirit.

As we serve, we will face resistance and rejection, just as Paul did. Second Timothy 3:12 says, "Everyone who wants to live a godly life in Christ Jesus will be persecuted," but we can rest assured that this suffering is not in vain. God is strengthening us, conforming us more to His Son, and preparing us for greater rewards in His kingdom.

While we may grow weary, Galatians 6:9 promises, "Let us not become weary in doing good, for at the proper time we will reap a harvest if we do not give up." This is a powerful affirmation to keep going even when the way is hard.

Ordinary People, Extraordinary God

Ultimately reflecting Christ is not about us—it's about Him. We become windows through which His light shines into a dark world. We become ordinary people used by an extraordinary God.

Therefore, let us pursue this high calling with patience, humility, perseverance, and a deep reliance on His Spirit. The world is in desperate need of an accurate reflection of our Lord, a reflection that brings healing, peace, and reconciliation.

The Simple Invitation: "Follow Me"

One of the simplest and most profound moments of calling in Scripture is found in Matthew 9:9: "As Jesus went on from there, he saw a man named Matthew sitting at the tax collector's booth. 'Follow me,' he told him, and Matthew got up and followed him."

This encounter is powerful in its simplicity. Jesus didn't require a résumé, a list of accomplishments, or even a confession of past mistakes. He simply extended an invitation: "Follow me." And Matthew, in faith, responded.

When Jesus calls us to represent Him, it's the same invitation. We are called not because we are qualified but because He chooses us. As with Matthew, we respond not with perfection but with willingness. Our role is to get up from where we are and begin walking with Jesus.

That first step of obedience is the beginning of a life that reflects Him. As with Matthew, we may leave behind things, status, comfort, and we definitely leave behind sin, but what we gain is far greater: a purpose rooted in Christ and a mission that changes eternity.

Reflection
Where in my life do I feel called to represent Christ more intentionally?
Am I staying connected to Jesus through prayer, or am I trying to represent Him in my own strength?
When people interact with me, do they walk away seeing Jesus?

Prayer
Jesus, I want to represent you well. Teach me to shine in a world that's dark. Keep me close to you in prayer so I don't drift into pride or performance. Let my life reflect your love, your truth, and your mercy.

Lord Jesus, help me reflect you in my life, in my words, in my choices, and in my relationships. Let others see your love through me. Help me walk in humility and truth, and when I fail, help me to repent quickly and return to you.

Use my life as a window into yours. Strengthen me to draw others to you, not because I am perfect but because I am yours. Help me serve with joy, love without limits, and trust you in every step.

I don't want to just claim your name, I want to live it daily.

In Jesus's name I pray. Amen.

Chapter 6

The Call to Follow Fully

There comes a point in every believer's life when Jesus doesn't just invite them to believe—He invites them also to surrender, not partially, not just when it's easy, but fully.

Jesus said in Luke 9:23, "Whoever wants to be my disciple must deny themselves and take up their cross daily and follow me." This isn't symbolic language. He meant it. This is the dividing line between casual Christianity and true discipleship.

Jesus Modeled Surrender First

But before we look at what that surrender means for us; we must first look at Jesus Himself. Long before He called any disciples, He modeled total surrender. He didn't just teach surrender—He also lived it.

As a child, Jesus had already showed a profound awareness of His Father's call. In Luke 2:49, when His parents found Him teaching in the temple at twelve years of age, He said, "Didn't you know I had to be in my Father's house?" Even then, He wasn't living for His own agenda but was submitted to the Father's will. And then He returned home and was obedient to His earthly parents, growing in wisdom, stature, and favor with God and man (Luke 2:52).

The Wilderness Prepares the Worker

Jesus didn't begin His public ministry until He was around thirty years old. That means He spent the vast majority of His life not on platforms, not performing miracles, not preaching to crowds—but simply obeying. Quietly. Patiently. Perfectly.

And when the time came to step out, Jesus didn't rush forward. He went into the wilderness first. For forty days He fasted and prayed—alone. And in that wilderness, He was tempted fiercely. Satan came after His identity, His authority, His hunger, and His mission. But Jesus didn't compromise. He responded with the Word, standing firm in surrender to His Father, showing us what preparation truly looks like.

If Jesus needed time in the wilderness before public ministry, how much more do *we* need time in surrender before full discipleship?

Letting Go of Control

The truth is—many of us want to follow Jesus but we don't want to let go. We want Jesus to walk with us, but we don't want to stop walking in our own direction. We want blessing but we hesitate at obedience.

That was my story. I believed in Jesus all my life. I knew He was real. I even served Him at times. But I didn't fully surrender. My life reflected that struggle: broken relationships, failed marriages, damaged priorities, and spiritual delays. I wanted to grow, but I wanted to keep control. And for years I walked the line between faith and flesh.

It took decades, nearly my entire adult life, to finally say, *Jesus, I give it all to you.* That surrender didn't erase my past, but it transformed my future. When I let go, God took hold. And that changed everything.

Counting the Cost of Discipleship

The rich young ruler understood the invitation and walked away from it. Mark 10:21 says, "Jesus looked at him and loved him. 'One thing you lack,' he said. 'Go, sell everything you have and give to the poor.. .. Then come, follow me.'" But the man couldn't do it. He wanted Jesus but not enough to lose his wealth, his comfort, his plan.

In Luke 14:28 Jesus reminds us to count the cost. "Suppose one of you wants to build a tower. Won't you first sit down and estimate the cost . . . ?" Following Jesus isn't just an emotional decision; it's a life-altering one. It will cost you. It may cost you status, relationships, dreams, addictions, comforts, habits, and pride. But the reward is greater than the cost.

The apostle Paul had everything: status, success, education, and respect. But in Philippians 3:8 he writes, "I consider everything a loss because of the surpassing worth of knowing Christ Jesus my Lord... I consider them garbage, that I may gain Christ." He didn't say that lightly. He had been beaten, imprisoned, betrayed, and rejected. And still he considered Jesus worth it all.

What It Means to Follow Fully

So what does it look like to follow fully?

To follow fully is to choose obedience before comfort—to worship when no one sees, to love people who don't love you back, to stay when you want to leave, to give when you don't feel like it, to pray when it feels dry, and to let go of anything that pulls your heart away from Him. Through it all, know that Jesus has already walked this road and that He walks it with you.

You may still be in the waiting, still in the wilderness, still learning how to surrender. That's okay. Don't rush it. But don't ignore it either. If the Spirit is tugging on your heart, listen. He's not trying to take something from you. He's trying to give something to you—a life of fruit, purpose, and peace.

Jesus said in John 15:16, "You did not choose me, but I chose you and appointed you so that you might go and bear fruit—fruit that will last." He chose you for more than just belief. He chose you also to follow—fully.

The call to follow Jesus fully is not for the faint of heart. It is a call to abandon comfort, pride, and personal ambition in exchange for a life of surrender. Jesus didn't soften the cost. He spoke plainly: to follow Him means denying yourself, taking up your cross daily, and walking in His footsteps. This isn't poetic language it's a real-life challenge to let go of everything that once defined us. True discipleship always begins with surrender. Many people admire Jesus, but far fewer follow Him. To follow fully means Jesus becomes not just Savior but also Lord, the one who directs your steps, your relationships, your goals, and your lifestyle.

One of the clearest examples of this is found in Mark 10:21, where Jesus speaks to the rich young ruler: "Go, sell everything you have and give to the poor, and you will have treasure in heaven. Then come, follow me." Jesus wasn't trying to take something away; He was offering a better treasure. But the young man walked away because the cost felt too high to him.

Following fully may mean giving up things that once felt essential. Not everyone is called to sell all his or her possessions, but we are all called to loosen our grip on anything that keeps us from Jesus. That could be money, career, reputation, entertainment, or even relationships that pull us away from God.

Obedience is not just about big sacrifices; it's also about daily decisions. Every day we are asked, *Will I follow my desires, or will I follow Jesus? Will I serve my comfort, or will I serve His kingdom?* These choices define the depth of our discipleship.

Sometimes following fully means going through seasons of isolation, discomfort, or pruning. John 15 reminds us that the Father prunes every branch that bears fruit so it can bear more. It can be painful, but it is always purposeful.

And Jesus doesn't call us just to follow Him blindly. He walks with us. In Matthew 28:20 He promised, "Surely I am with you always, to the very end of the age." Full surrender does not mean we walk alone, it means we walk with the King of kings, and we are not the first to walk this road.

When we look at the disciples, we see ordinary men who left their nets, their tax booths, and their former lives to follow Jesus. They were not superhumans. They were flawed, fearful, and unsure, but they said yes. That's what it means to follow fully: not perfection but surrender.

When Jesus calls us to follow Him fully, He also calls us to become disciple-makers. In Matthew 28:19 He commands, "Go and make disciples of all nations, baptizing them in the name of the Father and of the Son and of the Holy Spirit." This call is not just for the apostles but for every believer who has chosen to follow Him. To follow fully is also to lead others into the same journey. Our lives should naturally point others to Christ.

We live in a world full of distractions and detours. Every day something tries to steal our attention or slow our walk. But when we choose to follow Jesus above all else, He lights the path before us. In John 8:12 Jesus says, "I am the light of the world. Whoever follows me will never walk in darkness but will have the light of life." This isn't just about clarity—it's about direction, protection, and purpose. When we walk with Jesus, we don't stumble blindly through life. We walk with confidence, because the Light walks ahead of us.

This kind of full surrender isn't easy. In fact, it often costs us something: popularity, comfort, control. But it also brings us something the world can never give: peace, identity, and eternal purpose. In Luke 14:28 Jesus reminds us to count the cost of discipleship—not because He wants to discourage us but because He wants us to commit fully and understand the depth of what we're stepping into.

Think of the disciples again. They didn't fully understand everything when they first followed Jesus. They struggled, argued, doubted, and yet they stayed. And in staying they grew. They were transformed. And so will you. Following Jesus fully isn't about having it all figured out—it's about staying close enough to be changed by Him.

A fully surrendered life becomes a testimony. It shines in dark places. It brings hope to others. It builds the church. And most importantly, it pleases God. He isn't looking for flashy followers—He's looking for faithful ones, the ones who say yes when no one else will, the ones who show up, love well, and stay the course.

The Lifeline of Prayer Is Surrender

One of the greatest tools for walking in full surrender is prayer. Prayer is not just a habit—it's our lifeline. When we follow Jesus fully, we must remain in constant communion with Him. Jesus modeled this often, withdrawing to solitary places to pray (Luke 5:16). If He, the Son of God, prioritized prayer, how much more do we need it?

Prayer keeps us aligned with the Father's will. It strengthens us in weakness. It reminds us of who we are and whose we are. In seasons of confusion or discouragement, it is prayer that roots us back into the truth of God's promises. However, prayer is not just where we find strength; it is where we learn to surrender.

Surrendering fully means talking with God about everything: our dreams, our doubts, our mistakes, and our needs. It means listening, not just speaking. Prayer is where surrender becomes reality. It is where we say, "Not my will, but yours be done" (Luke 22:42).

When we neglect prayer, we become vulnerable to the pull of the world and the lies of the enemy. But when we pray, we stay close to the Shepherd's voice. We walk in the light. We are strengthened to obey, even when it's hard.

If you're serious about following Jesus fully, make prayer your anchor. Build your day around it. Set aside intentional time, but also invite God into the quiet, ordinary moments, the car rides, the chores, the pauses between conversations. He is always nearby. And He wants to walk with you.

When prayer becomes a lifestyle, surrender becomes a joy. Obedience becomes a response to love, not a burden. And following Jesus fully becomes the most natural path, even when it's the hardest one.

Reflection
What is Jesus asking me to lay down so I can follow Him more fully?

Am I still trying to keep control of areas I should have surrendered? What does a fully surrendered life look like for me?

Prayer

Lord, I don't want to follow you halfway. I want to follow you fully. Show me what I need to lay down. Teach me to walk in obedience, not just emotion. I surrender my plans, my pride, and my fears. Lead me and I will follow. You gave it all for me. Now I give it all to you. In Jesus's name. Amen.

Chapter 7

Becoming Like the Master

Once we've surrendered and committed to following Jesus, the next stage of discipleship begins: transformation. This is where God starts shaping us not just to believe like Jesus or serve like Him but to actually become like Him in our hearts, character, and lives.

First John 2:6 sets the tone clearly: "Whoever claims to live in him must live as Jesus did." The Christian life isn't about visiting Jesus on Sundays—it's about walking with Him daily, and your life will begin to reflecting His life.

But how does this transformation happen?

Christ Modeled Transformation Early

Jesus Himself showed us what spiritual growth looks like, even from a young age. As noted earlier, in Luke 2:46–52 we find Him at just twelve years old sitting in the temple courts, listening to the teachers and asking questions. When His parents finally found Him, He said, "Didn't you know I had to be in my Father's house?" (Luke 2:49). Even in childhood He was aligning His life with the Father's will.

By the time Jesus stood in the synagogue as a man in Luke 4, reading from the scroll of Isaiah and declaring, "Today this Scripture is fulfilled in your hearing" (v. 21), He wasn't just quoting truth—He was living it. That journey, from young learner to living embodiment, is the path every disciple walks.

You Were Made to Be Transformed

Romans 8:29 tells us that God's purpose is to conform us to the image of His Son. This isn't behavior modification. This is identity transformation. It means your mind starts thinking like Jesus. Your heart starts loving like Jesus. Your responses start reflecting Jesus.

It's slow. It's sacred. It's powerful.

But this change isn't something we can produce on our own. That's why Jesus said in John 14:26, "The Advocate, the Holy Spirit... will teach you all things." The Spirit isn't there just to convict or guide—He's there to *form* us, to teach us to walk like Christ from the inside out.

And let's be honest. The Spirit's teaching often takes us places we don't understand. But that's part of becoming like the Master. In John 13:7 Jesus said to Peter, "You do not realize now what I am doing, but later you will understand." Transformation requires trust, even when it's uncomfortable.

What Transformation Looks Like

Paul gives us the fruit of a transformed life in Galatians 5:22–23: "Love, joy, peace, forbearance, kindness, goodness, faithfulness, gentleness and self-control." These aren't tasks—they're fruit, evidence that the life of Jesus is growing in us.

Becoming like Jesus means—

Forgiving when you've been deeply wounded

Being patient with those who test your limits

Listening before speaking

Serving without expecting thanks

Speaking truth without harshness

Loving those who make it difficult

Let me paint a picture, not of a real person but of the kind of Christlike disciple many of us have seen or can become.

There was a woman we'll call "Grandma Elsie." She never taught a class, never stood on a stage. She sat quietly in the back row of church, always with a gentle smile. But every week people would come to her for prayer, for wisdom, for comfort—young women who had questions about faith, older folks who needed encouragement. She didn't have titles. But she had the Holy Spirit.

She would sit at her kitchen table in the morning, Bible open, praying over names scribbled in the margins. She gave hugs in a way that meant something. She never hurried people. She never tried to impress. But when you were around her, you felt as though you were around Jesus.

That's transformation.

That's discipleship.

That's what it means to become like the Master.

Becoming like Jesus Means Serving like Him

Ephesians 5:1–2 says, "Follow God's example . . . and walk in the way of love, just as Christ loved us and gave himself up for us as a fragrant offering and sacrifice to God." Becoming like Jesus means being willing to give of yourself, not because it's easy but because it's who He is.

And in Matthew 20:25–28 Jesus reminded His disciples that greatness isn't in position but in service. "Whoever wants to become great among you must be your servant," He said (v. 26). "The Son of Man did not come to be served, but to serve" (v. 28).

As you grow in Christ, your heart shifts from seeking status to seeking ways to serve others in love. This is what Jesus modeled throughout His life. He did not come to be served but to serve. He invited His followers to walk with the same humility and purpose. In John 13:14–15, after washing the disciples' feet, Jesus said, "Now that I, your Lord and Teacher, have washed your feet, you also should wash one another's feet. I have set you an example that you should do as I have done for you." This wasn't just about foot-washing. It was about heart posture. Jesus was showing them how to lead by lowering themselves. In a world that teaches us to rise above others, Jesus teaches us to kneel. Discipleship is not a climb to power—it's a descent into servanthood.

Philippians 2:5–8 urges us to adopt the same mindset as Christ, "Who, being in very nature God, did not consider equality with God something to be used to his own advantage… he humbled himself by becoming obedient to death—even death on a cross!" (vv. 6, 8). This radical humility is at the center of what it means to become like the Master.

Becoming like Jesus doesn't happen overnight. It's a daily transformation, a series of small choices: choosing grace over retaliation, patience over frustration, forgiveness when bitterness is easier. The Holy Spirit shapes us over time into the image of Christ.

We also become like the Master when we prioritize what He prioritized: time with the Father, compassion for the broken, truth in love, and a life marked by prayer and worship. Jesus often withdrew to pray, not because He needed a break but because He needed connection with the Father. So do we.

The world doesn't need more Christians in name only. It needs followers who carry the aroma of Christ in their speech, actions, and presence. People should feel seen, heard, and loved because they've been near us, just as they were with Jesus.

It's not always easy. Becoming like the Master will stretch you. It will bring conviction. It will mean loving your enemies, sacrificing your comfort, and putting others first. But in that process you will find joy unlike any other. You will begin to live with purpose, peace, and a love that surpasses understanding.

Pursuing the Lost like the Master

One of the most powerful illustrations of the heart of Jesus, and what we must reflect as His disciples, is found in Luke 15. In this chapter Jesus shares three parables: those of the lost sheep, the lost coin, and the lost son. Each story reflects the Father's overwhelming love for those who are far from Him and His desire for us to join in the search.

Jesus says in Luke 15:7, "There will be more rejoicing in heaven over one sinner who repents than over ninety-nine righteous persons who do not need to repent." As disciples, we're called not just to grow ourselves but also to go after the lost. Like the shepherd who leaves the ninety-nine to find the one, we must carry that same urgency and compassion.

It's easy to stay in our comfort zones, churches, small groups, and friend circles, but Jesus constantly stepped outside of comfort to reach the marginalized, the forgotten, the broken. And so must we.

Imagine a modern-day example: A disciple named Thomas regularly volunteers at a food pantry. One day a man named Andre walks in reeking of alcohol and cursing under his breath. Most people avoid him, but Thomas offers him a meal, looks him in the eye, and asks his name. Over weeks of simple kindness and honest conversations, Andre opens up about his past, his pain, and his longing for purpose. Eventually Andre gives his life to Christ and begins helping others who are struggling, all because one disciple decided to love like Jesus.

This is what it means to become like the Master. Jesus didn't avoid messy people—He loved them. He walked with them. He restored them. He never compromised truth but always led with grace.

We are called to do the same. Whether someone is rich or poor, clean or dirty, churched or unchurched—it doesn't matter. Every soul matters to God. If we are to become like Jesus, our love must not be selective. Our arms must be open.

This kind of love is costly. It requires time, patience, and sacrifice. But this is the very life Jesus modeled. And when we live this way, we become beacons of hope in a dark and divided world.

Spiritual Disciplines that Shape Us

Another vital aspect of becoming like Jesus is embracing His spiritual disciplines. Jesus didn't just preach—He practiced a deeply rooted, spiritually intimate life with the Father. He spent time in solitude, in silence, in prayer, and in the Word.

In Mark 1:35 we read, "Very early in the morning, while it was still dark, Jesus got up, left the house and went off to a solitary place, where he prayed." These rhythms of renewal sustained His ministry. For us to become like the Master, we must build our lives around these same rhythms.

Bible study renews the mind. Prayer transforms the heart. Fasting focuses the soul. Worship reminds us of who God is and who we are not. Silence and solitude draw us deeper into His voice and quiet the noise of the world.

To reflect Jesus outwardly, we must be shaped by Him inwardly. Disciples who neglect spiritual disciplines often find their faith growing thin, like a vine cut off from the source. But those who draw daily strength from God's presence shine with quiet authority and humble love.

Courageous Compassion: Truth and Love Together

Another key characteristic of Christ we must adopt is that of His courage. Jesus wasn't just gentle—He was bold. He stood for truth in a world full of lies. He called out injustice, confronted hypocrisy, and refused to compromise His mission. True discipleship doesn't hide behind fear. It speaks when it's easier to stay silent. It stands for righteousness even when it's costly.

Modern disciples are called to do the same. In today's world, truth is often twisted, and love is misunderstood. But those who become like the Master carry both truth and love as two sides of the same coin. They lead with compassion and follow through with conviction.

Becoming like Jesus Is Our Greatest Joy

Let us not forget that becoming like Jesus is not a burden. It is a joy and a privilege. It is the reason we were made to reflect God's glory, to embody His love, and to carry His mission forward. And every day we say yes to His shaping, we become more of who we were always meant to be.

Reflection

What part of Jesus's life or character do I most long to reflect?
Am I resisting the Spirit's shaping, or am I welcoming it?
Where can I serve more like Jesus—without needing recognition?

Prayer

Jesus, I don't want to just know about you—I want to become like you. Shape my life, my words, my thoughts, my heart. Teach me through your Spirit. Let your fruit grow in me. And let my life quietly reflect you, like a mirror turned to heaven. I'm willing, Lord. Make me more like you. Amen.

Chapter 8

Walking in His Footsteps

Discipleship isn't just about believing in Jesus. It's about walking in His footsteps, daily, humbly, intentionally. After surrendering to Christ and beginning to reflect His heart, the disciple enters a season of consistent growth and obedience. This chapter is about that season when your faith takes root and your life begins looking more and more like the life of your Master.

Aligning Your Life with His Example

First Peter 2:21 says, "To this you were called, because Christ suffered for you, leaving you an example, that you should follow in His steps." Following Jesus means aligning your pace, your path, and your posture to His. It means choosing daily disciplines that reflect His life and embracing the slow, beautiful process of becoming more like Him.

It doesn't happen in leaps and bounds. It happens in small, obedient steps.

The Foundation of Scripture

A disciple cannot walk with Jesus if he or she is not rooted in His Word. Scripture isn't just inspiration—it's instruction. As 2 Timothy 3:16–17 teaches, "All Scripture is God-breathed and is useful for teaching, rebuking, correcting and training in righteousness, so that the servant of God may be thoroughly equipped for every good work." If we are going to walk in His footsteps, we need to know where He walked, what He valued, how He responded, and what He taught.

This means carving out time to read, meditate, and let the Word soak into your daily thoughts and decisions. Scripture gives you the map, and when the road gets dark, it becomes your lamp (Psalm 119:105).

The Discipline of Prayer

Prayer is not just a ritual—it is your lifeline. It's the space where you commune with the one you're following. In fact, it's your lifeline between you and the Lord Jesus Christ.

Jesus showed us how vital prayer is. Luke 5:16 tells us, "Jesus often withdrew to lonely places and prayed." He didn't just pray in public or when He needed something—He prayed regularly, privately, intimately. Even at His most vulnerable moment in the garden, He said in Matthew 26:39, "My Father, if it is possible, may this cup be taken from me. Yet not as I will, but as you will."

When you walk in His footsteps, prayer becomes a pattern of surrender. It's where obedience is born and intimacy with God deepens.

The Power of God's Presence

Psalm 139:1, 3 reminds us that God knows our every step: "You have searched me, Lord, and you know me. . . .You are familiar with all my ways." Nothing you do is hidden from Him. That's not threatening—it's comforting. It means He walks with you, understands your struggles, and strengthens your obedience. And when you ask Him, He will search your heart and gently lead you in the way everlasting (Psalm 139:23–24).

Living Rooted and Built Up

Colossians 2:6–7 says, "So then, just as you received Christ Jesus as Lord, continue to live your lives in Him, rooted and built up in Him, strengthened in the faith." Discipleship is about remaining, not sprinting. You dig deep roots into Christ. You anchor yourself in spiritual rhythms. You build consistency.

This includes worship, private and corporate. It includes fellowship with other believers, accountability, and encouragement. Discipleship doesn't thrive in isolation. It grows in community.

New Creation, New Walk

Second Corinthians 5:17 says, "If anyone is in Christ, the new creation has come: The old has gone, the new is here!" Walking in His footsteps means letting go of who you used to be and embracing the new life Christ has given you. It's not about perfection. It's about direction. You're not walking to earn His love—you're walking because you've already received it.

The Mindset of the Master

Philippians 2:5 says, "In your relationships with one another, have the same mindset as Christ Jesus." Jesus' mindset was one of humility, service, patience, and surrender. He never rushed. He never sought power. He loved without condition and obeyed without hesitation.

This is the mindset that must take root in every disciple—not just in your theology but also in your tone, your decisions, your interactions, and your motives.

Walking in His Ways Today

To walk in His footsteps means to intentionally align every part of our lives with the way Jesus lived. This is not a poetic metaphor but a real calling, one that challenges us to let go of our own agendas and follow the rhythms and values of the Son of God.

Jesus's life was marked by complete submission to the Father. He said in John 5:19, "Very truly I tell you, the Son can do nothing by himself; he can do only what he sees his Father doing." Walking in His footsteps means listening, watching, and obeying just as Jesus did.

It means surrendering to Scripture, because the Word of God was central to everything Jesus taught and lived. If we want to walk as Jesus walked, we must be people of the Word.

Jesus's entire life was marked by obedience, even when it led to the cross. He didn't serve only when it was convenient. He loved people when they were difficult, healed when others ignored, and forgave even in His final moments on the cross.

To walk in His footsteps is to become familiar with sacrifice. We are called to deny ourselves, take up our crosses, and follow Him daily (Luke 9:23). This includes small, everyday decisions, how we spend our time, how we respond to frustration, how we treat others in moments when no one else is watching.

Jesus modeled what a Spirit-led life looked like. He often withdrew to lonely places to pray. He fasted. He worshiped. He fellowshipped with others. He grieved and rejoiced. He asked questions. He healed. He challenged. He embraced. And He did it all while staying perfectly in step with the Father.

God doesn't want just outward obedience; He wants our inner lives aligned with Christ. To walk in His footsteps is to live from the inside out, with a heart constantly open to His refining work.

Walking in His footsteps also means walking by faith, not by sight, not by convenience, not by comfort. In 2 Corinthians 5:7 Paul writes, "We live by faith, not by sight." Faith requires trust in God's timing, wisdom, and provision, even when we don't fully understand the path ahead.

John 1:7 says of John the Baptist, "He came as a witness to testify concerning that light, so that through him all might believe." Just like John, we are called to walk in the light and to bear witness to the one who is the Light of the World. Our lives must shine with the evidence that we have been with Jesus.

In Colossians 2:6 Paul writes, "Just as you received Christ Jesus as Lord, continue to live your lives in him." Discipleship is not a one-time decision; it is a daily walk, a journey, a consistent, intentional choosing to live as He lived, love as He loved, and obey as He obeyed.

Even when we walk through trials, the call remains the same. Psalm 23:4 offers this comfort: "Even though I walk through the darkest valley, I will fear no evil, for you are with me." Jesus never promised an easy walk, but He promised His presence. And that is enough.

In today's culture, walking like Jesus may look countercultural. It may mean forgiving when others seek revenge, serving when others seek to be served, listening instead of shouting, staying faithful when it's easier to quit. But this is the path that leads to life.

Discipleship is not about perfection—it's about progression. Every step taken in His direction is a step that shapes us. Some days the walk will feel bold and full of confidence. Other days it may feel slow and unsteady. But if we keep walking, we are growing.

So let us walk in His footsteps, with courage, conviction, and compassion, trusting that He who began a good work in us will carry it on to completion.

Transformation that Impacts Others

Walking in His footsteps transforms not only our behavior but also our very identity. Jesus doesn't just teach us what to do—He shows us who we are meant to be. We are not defined by our failures, past labels, or current limitations. We are disciples of the King, called to carry His presence into a broken world.

In John 15:5 Jesus says, "I am the vine; you are the branches. If you remain in me and I in you, you will bear much fruit; apart from me you can do nothing." This abiding relationship is at the core of discipleship. It's not about striving, it's about staying — staying connected to Him through prayer, Scripture, obedience, and surrender.

There is no true discipleship without transformation. Romans 12:1-2 challenges us to present our bodies as living sacrifices and to be transformed by the renewing of our minds. When we walk with

Jesus, we begin thinking differently, loving differently, living differently. We begin walking in grace and truth, just as our Master.

Consider a story: A young man named Elias was raised in a world of violence and brokenness. For years he was angry, believing he was worthless and forgotten. But one day someone shared the love of Christ with him, not just in words but through kindness, prayer, and patience. As Elias began walking with Jesus, everything changed. He learned to forgive. He started reading Scripture. He began mentoring other young men. Today he serves in ministry, a living testimony that Jesus doesn't just save, He transforms.

This is the kind of story that happens when we truly walk in His footsteps. We carry healing. We carry restoration. We carry the gospel, not just in our mouths but also in our manner. We become vessels of mercy in a world that desperately needs hope.

It won't always be easy. There will be ridicule, spiritual warfare, and even loneliness at times. But the reward is eternal. To walk in His footsteps is to walk the path of purpose, anchored in heaven but effective on earth.

So, walk boldly. Walk humbly. Walk faithfully. And know that every step taken in Jesus's footsteps draws you closer to becoming the disciple you were created to be.

There is another powerful example in Scripture of someone who walked in Jesus's footsteps even before knowing all the details of the gospel: the Roman centurion Cornelius. His story, found in Acts 10, shows what it looks like to walk in faith, humility, and spiritual hunger.

Cornelius was a Gentile and a Roman officer, yet he was described as a devout man who feared God, gave generously to the poor, and prayed regularly. He had not yet heard the full message of salvation, but he lived a life that honored God with the light he had been given.

Because of his faithful lifestyle, God sent an angel to him, and Peter was eventually brought into Cornelius's home to preach the gospel. What followed was extraordinary: The Holy Spirit came upon

Cornelius and his household even before baptism. It was a powerful confirmation that God looks at the heart, not status, background, or heritage.

Cornelius reminds us that discipleship is not about position, it's about posture. He was willing. He was open. He was obedient. And his faith impacted his entire household and community. Walking in Jesus's footsteps means living with that same readiness, a heart tuned to God's voice and a life that points others toward Christ.

Reflection

Walking in Jesus' footsteps is a lifelong commitment of surrender, love, and obedience. As you consider your own life, where are you walking today? Are you drawing closer to Him, or are you drifting? Are you inviting others to follow alongside you? True discipleship reflects the one we follow, in heart, attitude, and action.

Prayer

Jesus, I long to walk where you walk, to love as you love, and to serve as you served. Teach me to abide in you daily. Show me how to follow you more fully, in public and in private, in joy and in hardship. Make my life a living reflection of yours. Lead me and I will follow. In your name I pray. Amen.

Chapter 9

Living as a Disciple

To live as a disciple is not to live as a churchgoer or religious observer. It is to walk with Jesus daily, surrendered to His leadership, aligned with His Word, and transformed by His Spirit. A disciple doesn't simply believe in Christ but also follows Him.

Walking as Jesus Walked

First John 2:6 says, "Whoever claims to live in him must live as Jesus did." That's not a call to perfection—it's a call to imitation. Jesus loved the unlovable, forgave the undeserving, and obeyed the Father even unto death. That's the path of discipleship.

Peter, who once denied Christ three times, eventually became the bold preacher of Pentecost (Acts 2). What changed? He followed. He walked with Jesus, failed, was restored, and kept going. That's a disciple—not someone who never stumbles but someone who always returns.

Remaining in Him

Jesus said in John 15:4, "Remain in me, as I also remain in you. No branch can bear fruit by itself; it must remain in the vine." A disciple remains, through storms, temptations, delays, and victories. Remaining means abiding, and abiding means relationship.

The apostle John exemplified this well. Often called "the disciple whom Jesus loved," John remained close: at the Last Supper, at the cross, and later as a faithful witness in exile. He outlived the others not because of comfort but because of commitment. Disciples don't just start strong, they finish well.

Remaining isn't passive, it's intentional. It's prayer, Scripture, confession, correction, and staying close even when emotions fade. The disciple says, "I will not let go—because He has not let go of me."

The Fruit of a Disciple

Galatians 5:22–23 lays out the fruit of the Spirit: love, joy, peace, forbearance, kindness, goodness, faithfulness, gentleness, and self-control. These aren't personality traits—they're evidence that someone is walking in step with Jesus.

Paul's life is a living example. Once a persecutor of the church, his encounter with Christ on the road to Damascus changed everything (Acts 9). From that moment forward his life bore fruit in every way, in how he preached, how he endured persecution, and how he encouraged the church.

Disciples aren't measured by titles, sermons, or influence but by fruit. The Spirit of God will always produce the character of Christ in those who are truly following Him.

Love Is the Mark

In John 13:35 Jesus says, "By this everyone will know that you are my disciples, if you love one another." That's the clearest identifier, not how loud we sing, how much we know, or how busy we stay—but how we love.

Love in the life of a disciple shows up in sacrifice, in forgiveness, in humility. Paul wrote, "If I have a faith that can move mountains, but do not have love, I am nothing" (1 Corinthians 13:2). A true disciple loves deeply because he or she has been deeply loved.

Jesus loved the least, the lost, and the rejected. He loved those who couldn't give Him anything in return. That is what we must learn to do. That is the posture of a disciple.

Letting Your Light Shine

In Matthew 5:16 Jesus urges us, "Let your light shine before others, that they may see your good deeds and glorify your Father in heaven." A disciple doesn't live to impress—the disciple lives to glorify.

Paul let his light shine from prison cells and shipwrecks. Peter let his light shine in front of hostile rulers and skeptical crowds. His light didn't come from his own strength—it came from the Holy Spirit within.

Your light may shine in a hospital, a classroom, a kitchen, or a construction site. It may shine in forgiveness when others expect anger, in honesty when deception would be easier, or in joy when circumstances are bleak. Wherever you are, your life preaches.

The Cost of Living as a Disciple

Discipleship is not about ease, it's about endurance. Jesus never hid the cost. "Whoever wants to be my disciple must deny themselves and take up their cross daily and follow me" (Luke 9:23). This is a daily surrender, not a one-time prayer.

Peter paid the cost. He was beaten, imprisoned, and eventually crucified upside down. Paul was flogged, stoned, shipwrecked, and ultimately executed. John was exiled to Patmos. These weren't side stories; they are our blueprint. The original disciples didn't gain comfort—they gained Christ.

Modern discipleship may not always lead to death, but it always leads to sacrifice. It might mean surrendering your pride, reputation, or comfort. It might mean staying in a difficult place or walking away from something others applaud. But the reward is Christ Himself.

Disciples in the World Today

Discipleship is not just a first-century calling—it's a present-day mandate. And the world is watching. Many admire Jesus from a distance, but relatively few follow Him closely.

Being a disciple today means living against the grain, loving when others hate, serving when others seek power, obeying when others compromise. It means living by Scripture, not culture. It means standing for truth, even when it's unpopular.

And just as with the original disciples, you won't always get it right. But you keep coming back. You keep walking. You keep following.

A Disciple's Influence

A disciple never walks alone, because someone is always watching. Your life is a testimony. Your words carry weight. Your patience, peace, and presence can change an atmosphere.

The early church spread not just by sermons but also by lives. People saw the courage of Peter and John and "recognized that they had been with Jesus" (Acts 4:13). That's the mark we should leave—not titles but transformation.

Your influence may never make headlines, but it will be felt in heaven. That's what living as a disciple is all about.

A Disciple's Endurance

Endurance is one of the clearest marks of a true disciple. This was one of Paul's greatest teachings to the early church. In 2 Timothy 2:3 he wrote, "Join with me in suffering, like a good soldier of Christ Jesus." Discipleship isn't seasonal; it's steadfast. It's what keeps a believer pressing forward through hardship, disappointment, and spiritual drought.

The original disciples modeled this unshakable endurance. When threatened, imprisoned, and beaten, they did not quit, they rejoiced.

In Acts 5:41, after being flogged for preaching the name of Jesus, the apostles "left the Sanhedrin, rejoicing because they had been counted worthy of suffering disgrace for the Name." That is the heart of a disciple: faithfulness even under fire.

Paul endured beatings, shipwrecks, hunger, betrayal, and prison, not because he loved suffering but because he loved Christ more than comfort. He urged the church in Galatians 6:9, "Let us not become weary in doing good, for at the proper time we will reap a harvest if we do not give up." The disciple doesn't look for an escape route but keeps his or her eyes on eternity.

A Disciple's Message

Another powerful aspect of discipleship is the message we carry. Paul wrote in Romans 1:16, "I am not ashamed of the gospel, because it is the power of God that brings salvation to everyone who believes." The message of disciples isn't themselves; it's Jesus. And they carry that message into their homes, jobs, friendships, and communities.

Peter's boldness before the Sanhedrin in Acts 4 shows this clearly. After healing a beggar, he stood before religious leaders and declared, "Salvation is found in no one else, for there is no other name under heaven given to mankind by which we must be saved" (Acts 4:12). That kind of courage comes only from a heart transformed by the Holy Spirit.

The disciple speaks truth in love, not silence in fear. In today's culture, in which truth is often distorted and compromise is celebrated, the voice of a disciple must remain clear and unashamed—not angry or harsh but full of grace and truth, just as with Jesus (John 1:14).

Discipleship Multiplies

One of the final elements of true discipleship is this: it reproduces.

Disciples make disciples. Jesus didn't say, "Go and be a disciple." He said, "Go and make disciples of all nations" (Matthew 28:19). Discipleship is never just about you—it's about who comes after you.

Paul discipled Timothy. Peter mentored Mark. Barnabas encouraged Paul in his early ministry. The life of a disciple always reaches forward to help someone else rise. We teach what we know, but we reproduce who we are.

A mature disciple knows his or her life is seed and God will use it to grow fruit in others. That's why your life matters, even if you don't feel anyone is watching. People *are* watching. And what you model, someone else will follow.

Whether it's raising godly children, leading a Bible study, encouraging a friend in the faith, or simply living out your walk authentically, every faithful step you take invites someone else to come closer to Christ.

A Disciple's Daily Decisions

Discipleship is also shaped in the small decisions no one sees. Every morning that we choose Scripture over scrolling, prayer over panic, truth over convenience, we are choosing the way of Jesus. These moments don't always feel holy, but they are where transformation happens.

Jesus didn't just minister in crowds—He served one person at a time. He sat with individuals. He paused for the woman at the well. He noticed the touch of the woman with the issue of blood. He healed Jairus's daughter. He washed His disciples' feet. The disciple learns from Jesus not just in His teachings but also in His tenderness.

Paul reflected this kind of care in his ministry. In 1 Thessalonians 2:8 he wrote, "We loved you so much that we were delighted to share with you not only the gospel of God but our lives as well." That's discipleship—not just preaching truth but also walking with people in it.

A Disciple Is Teachable

Teachability is essential for every disciple. Peter was impulsive, bold, and often wrong, but he was teachable. He let Jesus correct him. He wept after denying Christ. He didn't let his failure be final. Instead, he followed again.

A teachable heart is one that welcomes growth, even when it's uncomfortable. Disciples don't cling to pride or image; they cling to Christ. Proverbs 9:9 says, "Instruct the wise and they will be wiser still." A disciple knows he or she has more to learn and will seek it out with humility.

Teachability keeps the heart soft and the mind open to correction, wisdom, and deeper understanding. Without it, growth stalls. With it, the Spirit can lead a disciple from one level of maturity to the next.

A Disciple's Identity Is in Christ

Perhaps most importantly, a disciple finds his or her identity in Christ, not in what he or she does, what others think, or how much he or she achieves. This was Paul's foundation. In Galatians 2:20 he said, "I have been crucified with Christ and I no longer live, but Christ lives in me."

A disciple is not driven by applause or recognition, does not serve to be seen. The disciple's strength comes from knowing that he or she belongs to Jesus, fully, permanently, and joyfully. That identity gives the disciple courage when criticized, endurance when overlooked, and joy when the cost is high.

We are not just followers—we are sons and daughters of the Most High God. From that truth we walk in confidence, humility, and freedom. The disciple doesn't strive to earn approval but walks because he or she is already loved.

Reflection
Am I walking in a way that reflects Jesus, not just in belief but also in behavior?
Do others see the fruit of the Spirit growing in my life?
Am I loving others the way Jesus loved me?
Where do I need to surrender more deeply so I can follow more faithfully?

Prayer
Lord Jesus,
Thank you for calling me not just to believe but also to follow. Help me walk as you walked — in humility, love, and truth. Teach me to abide in you, to bear lasting fruit, and to love when it's difficult. Strengthen me to carry my cross daily and shine for you in every space I enter. May my life reflect your light and bring glory to your name. Amen.

Chapter 10

Making Disciples

Jesus never meant for discipleship to end with us. From the beginning, His invitation to "follow Me" always came with the expectation that we would invite others to follow Him too. In this chapter we move from personal growth to multiplication, learning how disciples are called to make more disciples.

The Great Commission

Jesus said in Matthew 28:19–20, "Go and make disciples of all nations, baptizing them in the name of the Father and of the Son and of the Holy Spirit, and teaching them to obey everything I have commanded you. And surely, I am with you always, to the very end of the age."

This is the heart of disciple-making. It's not about growing churches or collecting converts—it's about leading others into a relationship with Jesus, walking with them, teaching them, and helping them grow in faith.

Jesus didn't say, "Go and make believers." He said, "Make disciples." There's a difference. Discipleship is about transformation, not just information. It's a journey, not just a decision.

Empowered to Witness

Acts 1:8 says, "You will receive power when the Holy Spirit comes on you; and you will be my witnesses . . . to the ends of the earth." Every disciple is a witness, someone who tells the truth about what he or she has seen, experienced, and come to believe.

We're not responsible for saving people—that's God's work. But we are responsible for sharing the truth, living it out, and pointing people to the Savior we know.

The Spirit gives us boldness, wisdom, and opportunity. Therefore, we must be faithful to say yes.

Every Believer Can Point to Jesus

Making disciples is not something reserved for experienced Christians, pastors, or missionaries. Every believer is part of this call. If you've met Jesus, you can introduce someone else to Him.

Even if you're new to the faith, even if you've been to church only once or twice, you can share what you've learned, what you've experienced, and why you're starting to walk with Jesus.

It's like the Samaritan woman in John 4, who told her whole village after meeting Jesus once; like Andrew, who told his brother Peter, "We have found the Messiah" (John 1:41). Their knowledge was small but their passion was big. And Jesus used them.

This means there is no excuse. You don't need to have all the answers—you just need to be real. When you share your journey, even in small ways, you're planting seeds that God can grow.

Modeling the Life of Christ

Paul said in 1 Corinthians 11:1, "Follow my example, as I follow the example of Christ." This is what disciple-making looks like: modeling Christ for others.

People learn more from watching than from listening. When you live out your faith, through love, humility, service, and grace, people notice. And when they ask questions, you have the chance to disciple them.

It's not about being perfect, it's about being available: real, humble, and consistent.

Reproducing Reproducers

Second Timothy 2:2 says, "The things you have heard me say . . . entrust to reliable people who will also be qualified to teach others." Discipleship is about reproduction.

You disciple someone so he or she can disciple someone else. This is how the gospel spreads, not just through pulpits but also through coffee shops, kitchen tables, text messages, and prayer walks.

When you lead a Bible study, when you check in with a new believer, when you invite someone to church, you are engaging in disciple-making.

It's not about a title—it's about a heart that says, "Follow me as I follow Jesus."

Living like the First Disciples

The original disciples of Jesus were not religious elites. They were fishermen, tax collectors, zealots, and ordinary men who were forever changed by an encounter with Christ. What marked them was not their background but their response.

When Jesus called Peter and Andrew, they left their nets immediately (Matthew 4:19–20). When He called James and John, they left their boat and their father. When He called Matthew, a tax collector, he left his booth and followed.

Their lives were forever changed—and not without cost. Peter was later crucified upside down for his faith. James, the brother of John, was the first of the apostles to be martyred. John was exiled to Patmos. Paul was beaten, stoned, and eventually executed in Rome.

And yet none of them turned back. Why? Because they understood that discipleship wasn't about safety, it was about surrender. It wasn't about comfort—it was about calling.

Paul and Timothy: A Model of Spiritual Reproduction

Paul did not just preach—he trained others. One of his greatest investments was Timothy, a young disciple he referred to as a son in the faith (1 Timothy 1:2). Paul mentored Timothy, traveled with him, and later entrusted him to lead churches.

This mentorship wasn't just about information—it was about imitation. Paul told the Philippians, "Whatever you have learned or received or heard from me, or seen in me, put it into practice" (Philippians 4:9). That's disciple-making.

In the same way, who are we raising up in the faith? Who are we mentoring? Who will lead when we're gone? This is the call of discipleship: not just to lead but to multiply.

Barnabas: The Encouraging Disciple-Maker

Barnabas was not one of the Twelve, but he played a powerful role in the early church. He mentored Paul when others feared him (Acts 9:27). He partnered with Paul on missionary journeys. He later discipled John Mark, even after Mark had failed.

Disciple-makers don't just teach—they restore. They lift others up. They believe in second chances. They walk with people long enough to see the fruit. We need more believers like Barnabas in the church today.

Priscilla and Aquila: Teaching with Clarity and Grace

In Acts 18 we meet Priscilla and Aquila, a husband-and-wife team who welcomed Apollos, a gifted speaker, into their home and "explained to him the way of God more accurately" (Acts 18:26).

They didn't confront him publicly. They didn't shame him. They discipled him in private, with love and truth. Apollos later became a powerful preacher of the gospel.

This is disciple-making in action: humble, relational, Spirit-led. Whether you're a couple, a parent, or a single believer, your home can become a place where disciples are made.

Mary Magdalene: A Devoted Disciple

Mary Magdalene is one of the most powerful and often overlooked examples of a true disciple. Luke 8:2 tells us that Jesus cast seven demons out of her, a woman once in deep bondage but now transformed by the mercy of Christ.

After her healing she followed Jesus faithfully. She helped support His ministry (Luke 8:3). She was present at the crucifixion when many had fled. And in John 20 she became the first person to witness the resurrected Christ and the first to proclaim the good news of His resurrection. Jesus entrusted the message of His victory over death to a woman once held by demons. That's redemption. That's discipleship

Mary Magdalene reminds us that no past is too dark for Jesus to redeem. And no follower is too unlikely for Him to use. She was a witness, a servant, a messenger, and a model for women and men today who are called to follow and proclaim Him.

What Their Lives Teach Us Today

What do all these examples show us? They show us that disciple-making is not a side activity. It is the Christian life.

As with Peter and John, we must be bold even in a hostile culture.
As with Paul, we must reproduce leaders, not just gather listeners.
As with Barnabas, we must see potential in those the world overlooks.
As with Priscilla and Aquila, we must teach with grace and humility.

These men and women gave their lives to the mission and the gospel exploded across the world because they did. Now it's our turn.

If you are a follower of Jesus, you are called to be a disciple. You don't need a seminary degree. You need surrender, Scripture, and the Holy Spirit. The rest is obedience.

The Cost of Discipleship: Then and Now

True discipleship has always come with a cost. Jesus Himself warned in Luke 14:27, "Whoever does not carry their cross and follow me cannot be my disciple." The early church knew this reality firsthand.

Stephen, a man full of faith and the Holy Spirit, became the first Christian martyr. In Acts 7 he boldly proclaimed the truth to the

Sanhedrin and, filled with the Spirit, saw the heavens open. Yet for speaking the truth he was stoned to death.

And watching it all, holding the coats of those who hurled the stones, was a man named Saul, who would later become Paul, the greatest disciple-maker of them all. Stephen's death planted seeds that would bear fruit in the life of a man who once persecuted the church.

Today disciples around the world still face persecution. In some countries they risk imprisonment, beatings, or death simply for gathering in Jesus's name. Others face rejection by family, job loss, or legal pressure.

In the West the cost may be more social than physical: ridicule, isolation, cultural pushback. But the principle is the same: to follow Jesus means to carry a cross.

Disciple-makers must be willing to lay down comfort, reputation, and control for the sake of the gospel.

The Power of Generational Discipleship

Paul's relationship with Timothy wasn't an exception—it was a pattern. In 2 Timothy 2:2, as noted earlier, Paul lays out the model of spiritual multiplication: "What you have heard from me . . . entrust to reliable people who will also be qualified to teach others."

This is four generations of faith:
Paul → Timothy → reliable people → others

This model is the heartbeat of church growth. Not crowds but reproduction, one life multiplied into many.

Who is your Timothy? Who is watching your example? Who will continue the mission when you're gone? That is the legacy of a disciple-maker.

Disciple-Making in a Hostile or Distracted Culture

The early church did not thrive because the world welcomed it. It thrived because disciples were faithful in a hostile world.

They discipled people in homes, in prisons, in catacombs, and marketplaces. They taught truth without compromise. They lived with radical joy and sacrificial love. And because of that, Christianity exploded across the Roman Empire.

Today we are surrounded by distractions, noise, comfort, and compromise. But the calling has not changed.

Now more than ever the world needs real disciples, men and women who will—
Speak the truth in love;
Live holy lives in private and public;
Invest in others not with information but with presence and prayer.

The harvest is plentiful, but the workers are few (Matthew 9:37–38).

Will you go into the field? Will you raise others up? Will you pass on what was entrusted to you?

A Final Call: You Are a Disciple-Maker

This isn't someone else's mission. It's yours.

If you've been saved by Jesus, you are called by Jesus—not just to grow but also to go, not just to believe but also to reproduce.

You are part of the same story as that of Peter, Paul, Barnabas, Timothy, Priscilla, and Aquila. Their mission is now your mission.

Don't wait until you feel ready. Start where you are. Be faithful with who's in front of you.

Teach what you know. Share what you've lived. Model what you follow. And trust the Spirit to do the rest.

You were not saved to sit—you were saved to multiply.

Go make disciples.

Reflection
Who in my life can I invest in spiritually?

Am I modeling Christ in a way that invites others to follow?
Do I believe that even my small testimony can make a big impact?

Prayer

Lord Jesus, thank you for calling me to be your disciple, and for trusting me to make more. Help me share my faith with boldness and humility. Help me to see those around me who need encouragement, teaching, and love. Make me a faithful reproducer, someone who lives out the truth and invites others to follow. Thank you for the people who discipled me. Now help me go and do the same. In Jesus's name. Amen.

Chapter 11

The Spirit-Led Life

Galatians 5:25 says, "Since we live by the Spirit, let us keep in step with the Spirit."

This means the Christian life is not just about receiving the Holy Spirit once—it's about walking with Him daily. To "keep in step" means to listen, to follow, to yield. The Spirit leads gently but firmly, nudging us in the direction of love, truth, and righteousness.

We see this in Jesus from the very beginning. Even as a child, He was drawn to His Father's presence. Even as a boy, Jesus was led by the Spirit to seek the Father.

Later, in Matthew 4:1, Scripture says, "Then Jesus was led by the Spirit into the wilderness to be tempted by the devil." The Spirit didn't lead Him into comfort. He led Him into a place of testing, growth, and spiritual victory.

If Jesus, the Son of God, followed the Spirit's leading in every decision, how much more do we need to?

To be Spirit-led means to stop relying on our feelings, our logic, or the crowd. It means learning to recognize the prompting of God within us and choosing to obey, even when it's hard.

Examples of Spirit-Led Obedience

Mary, the mother of Jesus, lived a Spirit-led life from the moment the angel appeared to her. When told she would give birth to the Son of God, her response was simple yet profound: "I am the Lord's servant. . .. May your word to me be fulfilled" (Luke 1:38). She didn't argue. She didn't panic. She simply surrendered.

Mary followed Jesus through every stage of His life, from His birth to His crucifixion. She pondered things in her heart, trusted God through mystery, and stood in the background with quiet faithfulness. She reminds us that being led by the Spirit is often about stillness, humility, and trust when we don't understand.

The life of another woman noted earlier, Mary Magdalene, shows what happens when the Spirit restores what was broken. Delivered from deep bondage (Luke 8:2), she lived with unwavering devotion to Christ. Her faithfulness kept her near when others fled, and her love opened her eyes to recognize the risen Lord first. She responded not out of obligation but because the Spirit had transformed her heart.

These women remind us that being Spirit-led isn't about platform—it's about presence. It's about proximity to Jesus. It's about saying yes when He calls, even in the dark.

The Roman centurion in Luke 7:1–10 showed what Spirit-led humility and faith look like. He approached Jesus not with pride but with deep reverence: "I do not deserve to have you come under my roof.. ... But say the word, and my servant will be healed" (vv. 6–7). Jesus marveled at his faith and healed the servant from a distance.

Another officer approached Jesus in John 4:46–54 and begged Him to heal his son. Jesus told him, "Go. Your son will live." The man believed the word and left. When he returned, he found that his son had been healed at the exact hour Jesus had spoken.

These men weren't Jews. They hadn't grown up with the law. But their hearts were tender. They were led by the Spirit to recognize the authority of Jesus. And their lives and those of their families were changed forever.

This is what it means to walk in the Spirit: to trust God's voice even when you can't see the answer, and to move forward in faith.

The story of the Good Samaritan in Luke 10 shows what it looks like to live a Spirit-led life of compassion. Others passed by the wounded man, but the Samaritan was moved by mercy. He responded to the need in front of him, even when it cost him something. That's the Spirit's voice, prompting us to stop, to act, to give.

The Spirit's Power in the Early Church

Then came Pentecost. In Acts 2 the disciples, who once hid in fear, were filled with the Holy Spirit. Peter, who had denied Jesus three times, stood up and boldly proclaimed the gospel to thousands. That day three thousand were saved.

This is what the Holy Spirit does. He transforms cowards into couriers of the gospel. He gives wisdom, boldness, clarity, and conviction. He doesn't just comfort—He commissions.

To live by the Spirit means—

Listening more than speaking;

Moving in faith instead of fear;

Obeying even when it's inconvenient.

It's trusting that God's promptings are better than our own plans.

The Spirit's Leading in Everyday Life

Sometimes the Spirit will lead us to speak boldly, as Peter did at Pentecost. Other times He'll tell us to be silent, as Jesus before His accusers. Sometimes He will lead us into wilderness seasons, as He did with Jesus. Other times He will lead us to a divine appointment, as He did with Philip and the Ethiopian eunuch in Acts 8.

Philip hadn't planned that moment. The Spirit told him to go south on the road to Gaza. He obeyed, and there he met a man reading Isaiah. Philip asked, "Do you understand what you are reading?" The man replied, "How can I, unless someone explains it to me?" And Philip, led by the Spirit, shared the gospel and baptized him.

This is what it means to be available. Philip wasn't trying to be impressive; he was trying to be obedient. That's the heart of a Spirit-led disciple.

Stephen, one of the early deacons, was another example. Full of the Spirit and wisdom, he spoke truth with power and grace. His final sermon in Acts 7 cut to the heart of the religious leaders, and they stoned him for it.

But even in death, Stephen was Spirit-led. He looked up and saw Jesus standing at the right hand of God. His last words echoed his Savior's: "Lord, do not hold this sin against them." He died in grace, not rage; in surrender, not bitterness.

Martyrdom didn't silence the church—it scattered it. And everywhere they went, those early believers shared the gospel. That's the Spirit's strategy. He multiplies through what the enemy means to destroy.

The Spirit-led life is not safe, but it is secure. It's not always comfortable, but it is always fruitful. Jesus didn't promise an easy road but promised His presence.

Romans 8:14 reminds us, "Those who are led by the Spirit of God are the children of God." This is our identity, not just as believers but also as Spirit-led sons and daughters of the King.

That same Spirit who hovered over the waters at creation now lives in us. That same Spirit who raised Christ from the dead now gives life to our mortal bodies (Romans 8:11). That same Spirit who gave boldness to Peter, love to Mary Magdalene, and peace to Stephen is at work in us today.

To be led by the Spirit is to live in daily dependence. It is to wake up with a simple prayer: *Holy Spirit, lead me today.* It is to surrender our need to control, to know, or to be perfect—and instead to trust that the one who began the work in us will carry it to completion.

Crossing Boundaries by the Spirit

Cornelius, a Roman centurion introduced in Acts 10 and referred to earlier, was not raised under the law of Moses. Yet he feared God, gave generously, and prayed faithfully. Though a Gentile under Roman rule, his heart was drawn toward the one true God.

For years he lived in obedience without the full picture of the gospel. He honored God with what he knew. He kept praying. He kept giving. He waited. His perseverance wasn't dramatic, but it was steady and sincere.

Then, in God's perfect timing, Peter was sent to his home. The gospel was preached. The Holy Spirit fell. Cornelius and his household were baptized. His quiet endurance opened a door for the gospel to spread beyond Israel, marking a pivotal moment in the early church.

Cornelius didn't write epistles or become an apostle, but his life speaks to every believer who is still waiting, still praying, still trusting. Sometimes perseverance means remaining faithful while the answers are still unfolding.

And God sees that kind of faith. He honors it. Faithful endurance is never wasted. And in Cornelius's case, that endurance didn't just bless his family, it changed the church forever. The Spirit broke boundaries, traditions, and expectations because one man dared to believe.

Living a Spirit-Led Life Today

Paul also had much to say about the Spirit-led life. In Galatians 5:16 he wrote, "So I say, walk by the Spirit, and you will not gratify the desires of the flesh." Then in verse 22 he outlined the fruit of the Spirit: "love, joy, peace, forbearance, kindness, goodness, faithfulness, gentleness and self-control." These qualities are not self-generated. They are the result of abiding in Christ and yielding to the Spirit.

Romans 8:5 says, "Those who live according to the flesh have their minds set on what the flesh desires; but those who live in accordance with the Spirit have their minds set on what the Spirit desires." This means our mindset and focus must shift. We must constantly tune our hearts to the frequency of heaven, rejecting the noise of the world.

In 1 Corinthians 2:12, Paul wrote, "What we have received is not the spirit of the world, but the Spirit who is from God, so that we may understand what God has freely given us." The Spirit enables us to comprehend spiritual truth, to hear God's voice, and to live wisely in a foolish world.

How does this apply today? Living a Spirit-led life might look like pausing in a conversation to pray before you speak. It might mean saying no to a promotion if it compromises your integrity. It might mean reaching out to someone you don't naturally connect with because the Spirit prompts you to show kindness.

It means checking your motives. Are you doing something out of ego, fear, and pressure, or out of obedience to God? Spirit-led living often goes against the grain of our culture. It invites us to be countercultural, not for the sake of rebellion but for the sake of righteousness.

The Holy Spirit may ask you to forgive someone who hasn't apologized, to serve when you would rather rest, to speak up when it would be easier to be silent. But every time we obey, we grow. We bear fruit. We reflect Christ.

This is not about perfection. It's about progression. As we walk by the Spirit, we become more like Jesus, formed in His image, filled with His love, led by His power.

Reflection

Am I trying to follow Jesus by my own strength or by the Spirit's power?

What areas of my life have I not surrendered to His leading?

Do I truly see myself as a vessel for God's will?

Prayer

Holy Spirit, I welcome you. Lead me, guide me, and shape me. Teach me to walk in step with you. Help me surrender my will and trust your voice. Let me be a vessel, not for my plans but for the will of God. I want to live the Spirit-led life, not just in moments but in everything. In Jesus's name I pray. Amen.

Chapter 12

Enduring in the Walk

The life of a disciple isn't always exciting or easy. There are seasons when the road is long, the wind is against you, and the finish line feels far away. In those moments, endurance becomes the mark of true discipleship. It is not emotional enthusiasm or outward success that proves a disciple's faith but rather faithful obedience over time.

Discipleship is not a sprint—it's a marathon. And only those who learn to endure will finish well. It's not the flashiest part of the journey, but it may be the most important. The early disciples understood this deeply. They didn't have only moments of glory—they lived lives of costly perseverance. And many of them endured to the very end, even unto death.

Do Not Grow Weary

Galatians 6:9 encourages us: "Let us not become weary in doing good, for at the proper time we will reap a harvest if we do not give up." These words from Paul are a lifeline to the weary disciple. Weariness is real. Even the strongest believers grow tired of doing what is right, especially when the fruit is not immediate. But Paul reminds us that God sees every step, every prayer, every act of obedience. The harvest is coming. Our job is to keep walking.

After denying Christ three times, Peter must have felt disqualified to continue. But Jesus restored him, not with condemnation but with commission. "Feed my sheep," Jesus said (John 21:17). Despite his past, Peter endured. He led the early church with boldness, even facing imprisonment and death. Tradition holds that Peter was crucified upside down for his faith. He finished his race—not because he was perfect but because he endured.

Joy in the Trials

James 1:2–3 says, "Consider it pure joy, my brothers and sisters, whenever you face trials of many kinds, because you know that the testing of your faith produces perseverance."

Endurance is forged in trials. It doesn't grow in comfort. God uses pressure to strengthen our spiritual muscles. What we want to escape, God often uses to equip. The cross was not a detour in Jesus's mission—it was the very road to glory. And so, it is with us.

Paul endured stonings, beatings, shipwrecks, hunger, and prison (2 Corinthians 11:23–27). Yet he said in Romans 5:3–4, "We glory in our sufferings, because we know that suffering produces perseverance; perseverance, character; and character, hope." Paul's life teaches us that trials are not evidence that God is absent—rather, they are opportunities to cling to Him more deeply.

Joy in trials doesn't mean pretending everything's fine, it means recognizing that even the struggle has purpose. Every hardship is a refining fire, burning away pride, selfishness, and fear and making us look more like Christ.

Run with Perseverance

Hebrews 12:1–2 calls us to endurance: "Let us run with perseverance the race marked out for us, fixing our eyes on Jesus, the pioneer and perfecter of faith." Each of us has a race to run. Each of us has a calling to fulfill. But not everyone finishes well. Those who do are the ones who press forward when the path grows difficult.

Perseverance isn't glamorous. It's quiet faithfulness in the unseen moments. It looks like praying when you're tired, reading Scripture when it feels dry, serving when it's inconvenient, and choosing obedience over comfort.

One of the clearest examples of such perseverance is Mary, the mother of Jesus. Her endurance was not loud or dramatic but steady and steadfast. She bore the perceived scandal of carrying the Messiah. She fled with Joseph to Egypt to protect her newborn child from Herod's wrath. She stood at the cross when others fled, watching her Son suffer and die. Through every heartbreak she remained faithful. Mary's story reminds us that true strength is found not in noise or recognition but in loyal, unwavering love.

Pressing toward the Goal

Philippians 3:14 says, "I press on toward the goal to win the prize for which God has called me heavenward in Christ Jesus." Disciples don't live for this world; they live for eternity. The reason we keep going is not because it's easy but because the prize is worth it—the presence of Jesus. The "well done" is the eternal reward.

Paul didn't press on because he was strong—he pressed on because he was called. And so are we. Jesus never promised ease, but He did promise His presence. The road of endurance is not walked alone.

When You're Running on Empty

Sometimes, despite our best efforts, we feel as if we can't go any farther. Spiritual burnout is real. That's when we return to the basics: rest, prayer, worship, Scripture, and community.

Jesus Himself modeled this. He often withdrew to lonely places to pray (Luke 5:16). He rested. He took time with the Father.

Take a break *with* God, not *from* God. Rest isn't quitting—it's repositioning. Worship in the silence. Pray with no words. Read Scripture slowly and let the Word read you.

Lean on others. Find a small group. Share the burden. Let someone else walk with you when your legs are weak. Barnabas, whose name means "Son of Encouragement," walked alongside Paul and Mark when they needed someone to believe in them. We all need Barnabas friends, and we are called to be that for others too.

The Discipline that Fuels Endurance

To endure well, a disciple must develop habits that fuel the soul. This includes—

Daily prayer—your lifeline to the Father, Son, and Holy Spirit

Scripture meditation—food for your journey

Fellowship—encouragement and accountability from other believers

Worship—recentering your heart on God's greatness

Fasting—clearing distractions to focus more fully on Him

These disciplines are not burdens; they are fuel. Without them we drift. With them we thrive. Spiritual endurance does not come by accident—it grows through intentional surrender.

Stephen: Enduring to the End

Stephen, full of the Holy Spirit, stood firm in the face of death. In Acts 7 he preached the truth with boldness and was stoned for it. Yet even in death he forgave his killers and saw the heavens open. Jesus stood to receive him. Stephen's endurance was eternal in focus and Spirit-empowered. He didn't live long, but he lived faithfully. And his death sparked a movement that scattered the church and spread the gospel.

Joseph: Faithful in the Waiting

Joseph's story in Genesis is one of the clearest pictures of endurance in Scripture. Betrayed by his brothers, sold into slavery, and falsely imprisoned, Joseph spent years waiting on God's promises to come to pass. Yet through every trial he remained faithful. He honored God in Potiphar's house, in prison, and later in Pharaoh's courts. Joseph's endurance was not passive. It was patient trust. And in God's time his waiting gave way to purpose.

Keep Going

You do not have to run fast; you just have to keep running. The path is marked out for you, and God runs with you. Discipleship is about persistence. It is waking up again tomorrow and saying, "Yes, Lord. I'm still following." This is how we finish well, not in bursts of passion but in steady steps of faith. This is how we endure in the walk, one obedient step at a time.

Even Jesus Had to Endure

Jesus's time in the wilderness was not a pause in His mission; it was preparation for it. Before He preached a single sermon or healed a single person, He endured testing that shaped His walk. In the same way, our wilderness seasons are not wasted. God uses them to strengthen our character, deepen our trust, and prepare us for what lies ahead. Jesus shows us that endurance is not weakness but rather faithfulness under pressure. And as we endure, we are shaped by the same Spirit, strengthened by the same Word, and made more like Him.

Endurance in Gethsemane and the Cross

Perhaps the greatest picture of endurance is found in the Garden of Gethsemane Luke 22:44 tells us, "And being in anguish, He prayed more earnestly, and His sweat was like drops of blood falling to the ground." Jesus was not numb; He was in deep emotional and spiritual agony. And yet He didn't run. He prayed, "Not my will but yours be done." He chose obedience over escape.

Then came the cross. Betrayed, beaten, and mocked, Jesus carried the weight of the world's sin. Hebrews 12:2 says, "For the joy set before him he endured the cross, scorning its shame, and sat down at the right hand of the throne of God."

Jesus endured, not because it was easy but because it was necessary. He shows us that endurance is rooted in love: love for the Father and love for us. He stayed and suffered so that we could be saved. In the same way, we endure not to earn anything but because we are following in His footsteps.

Paul: Endurance Fueled by Calling

Paul's life was marked by challenges, but what carried him forward was his calling in Christ. He endured not because the path was easy but because the mission was worth it. His strength came from the Spirit of God who sustained him through every season of ministry.

When Paul told Timothy, "I have fought the good fight, I have finished the race, I have kept the faith" (2 Timothy 4:7), he was pointing to the faithfulness of God, who equipped him to finish well. Paul's story reminds us that endurance is not about surviving hardship—it is about remaining faithful to the work God gives us until the very end.

Enduring When No One Sees

Some of the hardest endurance is the kind no one notices: the mom who keeps praying for her wayward child, the man who keeps going to work even when he feels unseen, the student who chooses holiness over popularity, the elderly believer who keeps reading God's Word even when the world forgets him or her.

These are the quiet saints. Their endurance doesn't make headlines, but it fills heaven with joy. Hebrews 6:10 reminds us, "God is not unjust; he will not forget your work and the love you have shown him."

God sees every step, every tear, hears every quiet prayer. And He is faithful to reward those who do not give up.

Encouragement from Fellow Disciples

Peter's journey reminds us that failure is not the end of our story. Though he denied Jesus three times, the risen Christ restored him and called him to feed His sheep. Peter did not let shame define him. He received grace and kept walking. In time, he became one of the boldest voices for the gospel, enduring imprisonment and persecution for Christ's name.

John, "the beloved disciple," faced his own trials. He witnessed the loss of his closest friends and the suffering of the early church. Exiled on the island of Patmos, far from comfort and community, John remained faithful. It was there in isolation that he received the Revelation, a vision of hope for all who endure.

These men show us that endurance is not about perfection—it is about returning to Jesus again and again, trusting His grace and standing firm until the end.

Reflection

Am I weary in doing good? Where do I need strength?

What trial is God using to produce endurance in me?

Is my prayer life fueling my perseverance or am I running on empty?

Which discipline do I need to renew to strengthen my walk?

Prayer
Father, help me not to give up. Jesus, help me to press on. Holy Spirit, strengthen me to endure. Teach me to run with perseverance and not grow weary. Remind me that the prize is worth it and that you are with me every step of the way. I trust you to carry me through the long journey. In Jesus's name. Amen.

Bonus Prayer for the Weary Disciple
Lord, I'm tired. My soul is dry. Fill me again with your strength. Breathe life into my spirit. Rekindle my fire. Help me to rest in you, walk with you, and not give up. Thank you for staying with me even when I struggle. I need you. I trust you. I love you. In Jesus's name. amen.

Chapter 13

Perseverance

The Christian life isn't measured by how you start; it's measured by how you finish. Perseverance is what carries a disciple from that first step of faith to his or her final breath. It's not glamorous. It's not easy. But it's powerful.

When storms rise, when the road grows steep, when others fall away, perseverance keeps your eyes fixed on Jesus. It's the steady courage to keep trusting, keep walking, and keep believing, even when everything around you says, "Just quit."

Perseverance is not a one-time decision. It's a daily choice: Jesus over comfort, faith over fear, obedience over convenience. It is the quiet, unwavering evidence that Christ truly lives in us.

Blessed Are the Steadfast

James 1:12 says, "Blessed is the one who perseveres under trial because, having stood the test, that person will receive the crown of life that the Lord has promised to those who love him."

God doesn't reward ease, comfort, or talent. He blesses the one who stood when it was hard, the one who kept believing through pain, the one who stayed faithful when it would have been easier to walk away.

This "crown of life" isn't given for spiritual performance—it's promised to those who endure. That's what makes it beautiful. It's not earned through ease but through faith that refused to quit.

Perseverance isn't flashy. It doesn't always look strong. Sometimes it's quiet tears, whispered prayers, and shaky steps forward. But God sees it. And He honors it. In His kingdom perseverance produces fruit that nothing else can.

Jesus affirmed this in Luke 8:15, saying the good soil is the one who hears the Word, holds it, "and by persevering produce[s] a crop." The deepest growth comes not from excitement but from endurance.

So, if the road is long and your strength feels small, don't let go. God sees your perseverance. And He calls you blessed.

Trouble Is Part of the Journey

Jesus said in John 16:33, "In this world you will have trouble. But take heart! I have overcome the world." Trouble isn't the exception; it's part of the journey. Trials don't mean you've done something wrong. They often mean you're walking with Jesus in a world that resists Him.

Peter knew this firsthand. He once vowed never to fall away, but on the night Jesus was arrested, he denied Him three times. He wept bitterly in shame. Yet Jesus didn't cast him aside—He restored him. "Feed My sheep," He said. And Peter did. He led the early church, preached with boldness, and endured imprisonment, beatings, and ultimately death on a cross.

Peter didn't persevere because he was strong. He endured because he leaned on the mercy and mission of Jesus more than on his own strength.

Perseverance begins where comfort ends. That's often where real transformation begins. Trials strip away what's shallow and force us to cling to what's eternal.

So, if the pressure feels heavy and your strength feels small, don't assume you're failing. You may be right where God wants to build something unshakable in you.

Perseverance Builds Character

Romans 5:3–4, noted earlier, reminds us, "We also glory in our sufferings, because we know that suffering produces perseverance; perseverance, character; and character, hope."

We often pray for God to take the suffering away, but He often chooses to use it instead. Through hardship He teaches us endurance. Through endurance He shapes our identity. And through the refining fire He forms the likeness of His Son in us.

Paul, who penned these words, knew suffering intimately: beatings, shipwrecks, hunger, and prison. And yet he never walked away from his calling. Every affliction drove him deeper into grace, and out of that grace came resilience, joy, and an eternal mindset.

This is how character is formed, not in comfort but in perseverance. When we keep walking with Christ through trials, we don't just survive—we are transformed.

The Disciples after the Resurrection

The original disciples didn't become bold overnight. After Jesus was crucified, they were afraid, scattered, and uncertain. But the resurrection changed everything, and Pentecost ignited their courage.

Each of them lived a life marked by perseverance. They didn't walk with Jesus just during His ministry—they continued after His ascension through hardship, persecution, and death. They became the spiritual foundation of the church not because they were flawless but because they endured to the end.

- Peter was crucified upside down.
- John was exiled to Patmos, still proclaiming truth as he wrote Revelation.
- James was beheaded in Jerusalem, the first apostolic martyr.
- Andrew was crucified on an X-shaped cross, preaching as he died.
- Thomas carried the gospel to India and was killed by a spear.
- Bartholomew was reportedly flayed and then beheaded.
- Matthew preached in Ethiopia and was killed by the sword.
- Philip, Simon the Zealot, Jude, and others suffered similar fates.

They weren't naturally fearless, they became faithful. Their strength came not from within but from above. The Spirit of God transformed them, and they held fast through every trial.

Their lives preach one message: perseverance is not just surviving—it is staying faithful to Jesus no matter the cost.

You Need to Persevere

Hebrews 10:36 says, "You need to persevere so that when you have done the will of God, you will receive what he has promised."

Perseverance is not a spiritual suggestion. It's a requirement. God's promises are sure, but they often are found on the far side of trials. His will is not always fast or easy, but it is always worth it.

When you're tired, keep going. When the path feels unclear, keep praying. When your strength is gone, lean on the one who never grows weary. He is not asking you to be impressive, just faithful.

You may not always feel strong, but a persevering disciple is already victorious in heaven's eyes. God crowns the ones who endure.

So, stay the course. Endurance isn't just about getting through. It's how we walk through trials while still trusting the one who called us.

They Became Our Teachers

The disciples were more than followers. They became living examples of perseverance for every believer who would come after them. Through their letters, their obedience under pressure, and their faith through suffering they showed us what endurance looks like.

They didn't just talk about perseverance, they lived it. Mocked, beaten, imprisoned, and exiled, they kept going. Their faith wasn't proven in comfort but in hardship.

These weren't polished messengers speaking from a distance. Many of their words were written in chains, shaped by pain, and refined by fire. Yet they still encouraged others to press on.

Their lives now teach us that faith is not just for the mountaintop, but for the valleys too. They remind every weary disciple: You are not alone. Others have walked this path and it's worth it to keep going.

Peter: From Denial to Devotion

Peter's story may be the most personal example of perseverance among the disciples. Bold in speech but weak in the moment, he denied Jesus three times on the night of His arrest. As the rooster crowed, Peter locked eyes with the Savior he had just disowned and fled, weeping bitterly (Luke 22:61–62). His confidence was shattered, his failure complete.

But Jesus wasn't finished with Peter.

After the resurrection Jesus met him not with shame but with restoration. Beside a fire, just like the one where Peter had denied Him, Jesus asked three identical questions: "Do you love me?" And three times Peter responded. With each answer Jesus recommissioned him: "Feed My sheep" (John 21:15–17). It wasn't just forgiveness, it was renewal. Jesus gave him back his purpose.

Peter's life changed from that moment on. He preached boldly at Pentecost. He led the early church through persecution. He was arrested, beaten, and eventually crucified upside down, counting himself unworthy to die the same way as his Lord.

Peter persevered not because he was perfect. He endured because grace met him in his failure and the Holy Spirit filled what had once been broken.

And if Jesus did that for Peter, He can do it for you.

Every disciple stumbles. But the ones who finish well are the ones who get back up, again and again trusting the one who still says, "Follow me."

Keep walking. Grace has already gone ahead of you. The race is still yours to run.

Persevering through the Silence

After the crucifixion the disciples entered their darkest hours. Their Master was gone. Their hopes were shattered. Their future felt lost. Behind locked doors they sat gripped by fear (John 20:19), overwhelmed by silence. The one they had followed, trusted, and loved now lay in a tomb. Everything they had left behind to follow Him seemed to have led to nothing.

In those three days there was no visible victory, no miracle in sight—only silence. All they had were His words, and even those felt distant. This is often the hardest kind of perseverance: holding on in the dark, trusting what God said when there's no sign of what He's doing.

But then came the resurrection.

Jesus didn't rebuke them for hiding. He entered the room and breathed peace over their fear. He didn't just calm their panic; He reignited their purpose. From that moment forward they never looked back.

The same men who once fled would now follow to the very end. And they would do it with a fierce and faithful endurance that turned the world upside down.

Jesus Persevered for Us

The greatest example of perseverance is found not in the disciples but in Jesus.

He endured what no one else could: betrayal by a friend, abandonment by His followers, false accusations, mocking, beating, and crucifixion. He bore the weight of sin while being ridiculed by the very ones He came to save.

But He did not turn back. He did not give up.

He endured the wilderness, forty days of fasting and temptation, yet remained without sin (Matthew 4:1–11). He endured rejection from His own people. He endured Gethsemane, where His soul was overwhelmed, and His sweat fell like drops of blood (Luke 22:44). He endured the cross, shame, pain, and mockery because of the joy set before Him.

Hebrews 12:2 says, "For the joy set before Him, He endured the cross, scorning its shame, and sat down at the right hand of the throne of God." That joy was us, redeemed, restored, and reconciled to the Father.

He carried His cross through the streets of Jerusalem, climbed the hill of Golgotha, and took our place. Then He went further still, through the grave, and rose on the third day, victorious over death and the powers of darkness.

Jesus didn't stay on the cross because He was powerless. He stayed because He was faithful. His obedience flowed not from ease but from love. He finished what the Father had sent Him to do.

When you feel weary, misunderstood, or ready to quit, look to Him. When your strength is gone, remember His. Jesus finished His race so we could run ours. And now through His Spirit He walks with us every step of the way.

Be Joyful, Patient, and Faithful

Romans 12:12 offers a simple yet powerful guide to perseverance: "Be joyful in hope, patient in affliction, faithful in prayer."

These are not casual suggestions—they're the lifelines that sustain us when the road is long.

Joyful in hope—not because circumstances are easy but because our eternity is secure. Joy is anchored in the victory of Christ, not the moment we're in. Hope lifts our eyes and reminds us that our story ends in glory, not defeat.

Patient in affliction—because trials are temporary, but God's work in us is eternal. Patience isn't passive—it's the choice to trust when nothing makes sense, to hold your ground when you would rather run, and to believe that God is still working, even in the silence.

Faithful in prayer—because perseverance doesn't come from willpower. It comes from God. Prayer keeps us connected to the one who strengthens and sustains. It's not just for desperation—it's the steady rhythm of discipleship.

Perseverance doesn't always look bold. Sometimes it looks like tears. Sometimes it looks like silence. But in heaven's eyes every quiet act of trust matters. Every time you choose faith over fear, prayer over panic, and obedience over ease, you're walking the path Jesus walked. And He sees every step.

Paul: The Persevering Disciple

Paul's life was marked by relentless endurance. He was beaten, stoned, shipwrecked, imprisoned, betrayed, and often left in weakness. Yet he never walked away from the calling of Christ.

In 2 Corinthians 11:24–27 Paul listed his many trials, not for sympathy but to show the cost of faithful discipleship. His goal was never comfort but rather obedience. Even in suffering Paul pressed forward. He preached, planted churches, wrote letters, and encouraged believers with his eyes fixed on eternity.

At the end of his journey Paul wrote, "I have fought the good fight, I have finished the race, I have kept the faith" (2 Timothy 4:7). That is perseverance—not perfection but daily faithfulness. Not applause but unwavering obedience until the end.

Paul poured out his life for the gospel. And now his legacy calls us to do the same—to keep going, keep trusting, and never give up.

Endurance in the Shadows

Some of the most powerful acts of perseverance happen in places no one sees, not on stages or behind pulpits but in kitchens, bedrooms, quiet offices, and worn prayer chairs.

It's the elderly saint who still rises early to pray, even when his or her hands tremble and the days are long. It's the mother who opens the Word with her children even when she feels invisible. It's the man who quietly chooses integrity, resists temptation, and loves his family without recognition or applause.

These lives may never be broadcast, but heaven sees them clearly. Hebrews 6:10 reminds us, "God is not unjust; he will not forget your work and the love you have shown him."

This is the perseverance of the hidden servant, the disciple who remains faithful in the small things, in quiet places, through long seasons when no one is watching. Their strength isn't celebrated by the world but is honored by the Lord.

Not all perseverance is public. Some of the deepest faith grows in silence. And when no one else sees, God does. He remembers every unseen prayer, every quiet surrender, every faithful step.

When you feel invisible, know this: God is not blind to your faithfulness. The crown of life isn't given to the loud or the well-known. It's promised to the faithful.

Keep Going

You don't have to be fast. You don't have to be strong. You must simply keep going, one step at a time, one prayer at a time, and one day at a time.

Some days the road will feel long. Your strength may feel small. But that's when perseverance shines. Keep walking. Keep believing. Lean on the one who never lets go.

The race isn't won by talent or speed but by those who refuse to quit, those who fall and rise again, those who endure.

Galatians 6:9 encourages us, "Let us not become weary in doing good, for at the proper time we will reap a harvest if we do not give up."

That's the promise—not ease but reward, not comfort but a crown, not recognition but eternal joy in the presence of the one who sees it all.
Keep going. The finish line is ahead, and you are not running alone.

Reflection

Have I considered giving up when the path of faith grew difficult?

What does the perseverance of the original disciples teach me about following Jesus?

In what area of my life do I need to grow in patience, hope, or endurance?

What quiet acts of faith am I offering that only God sees? Am I trusting that He sees them?

Prayer

Father, I want to finish well. When trials press in, help me stand firm. When doubt creeps in, help me trust your Word. When I am weary, strengthen me by your Spirit. Thank you for the faithful examples of those who have endured before me, who followed you to the end. Fill me with that same perseverance. Keep my eyes on Jesus. I want to walk with you all the way home. In Jesus's name. Amen.

Chapter 14

The Journey Continues

The walk of a disciple doesn't end with a moment of belief or a baptism. It is a lifelong journey of transformation, obedience, and surrender. Becoming a Christian is the beginning of the path, but becoming a disciple means choosing each day to follow Jesus wherever He leads.

That choice is not made once—it is made again and again. The journey continues after the altar call. It continues after the excitement of new faith fades. It continues in the quiet seasons, the difficult seasons, and the hidden places where no one applauds except heaven. Discipleship is not a single event—it is a life lived in the footsteps of the Master.

This is the invitation of Jesus: "Follow me"—not for a moment but for a lifetime, through mountains and valleys, through joy and sorrow, through growth and pruning. The path of a disciple may be narrow, but it is filled with the presence of Christ. And it continues until the day we see Him face to face.

Keep Walking

The Christian life is often described as a walk, not a sprint. In Colossians 2:6 Paul writes, "Just as you received Christ Jesus as Lord, continue to live your lives in him." Some translations say, "walk in Him." The walk implies steady, forward movement, not perfection but progression. The disciple keeps walking, keeps trusting, keeps pressing forward.

John the apostle, one of Jesus's closest friends, began his journey as a fiery, ambitious young man. He and his brother James were called the "sons of thunder" (Mark 3:17). But as he walked with Jesus through miracles, teaching, betrayal, the cross, and the resurrection,

John was transformed. By the time he wrote his gospel and epistles, John was known not for thunder but for love. He became the apostle who taught the church to walk in truth and love (2 John 1:6). His journey didn't end at the cross but continued through exile on Patmos, where he received the revelation of Christ.

Discipleship is a path of becoming, of maturing, of going deeper in faith and higher in purpose. You don't stay where you started — you keep walking.

You Haven't Arrived Yet

Paul, after years of ministry, miracles, and missionary journeys, still said, "Not that I have already obtained all this . . . but I press on to take hold of that for which Christ Jesus took hold of me" (Philippians 3:12). If Paul hadn't arrived yet, we haven't either.

That's the heart of discipleship. It's not about reaching a finish line early—it's about pressing on. Discipleship doesn't end with spiritual achievement. It continues through spiritual hunger. The disciple is never content to sit still; he or she longs to know Jesus more deeply, follow Him more closely, and reflect Him more clearly.

That's why Paul also wrote in Philippians 1:6, "He who began a good work in you will carry it on to completion until the day of Christ Jesus." God didn't just save us—He is sanctifying us, shaping us, and strengthening us day by day. The journey continues because God's work in us is not finished.

The Road Is Narrow

Jesus told His followers in Matthew 7:13–14, "Enter through the narrow gate. For wide is the gate and broad is the road that leads to destruction. . . .. But small is the gate and narrow the road that leads to life, and only a few find it."

The journey of discipleship doesn't follow the crowd. It often leads against the flow of the world. It demands sacrifice. It confronts sin. It asks for everything. But it gives eternal life.

Peter understood this narrow road well. After denying Jesus three times, he was restored and continued his journey with renewed fire. Peter stood boldly before religious leaders who had crucified Jesus and said, "We must obey God rather than human beings!" (Acts 5:29). His journey was not without missteps, but he stayed on the road. Even in weakness he pressed forward.

That is the disciple's call: to keep walking the narrow road even when it's lonely or steep, even when others turn back.

The Holy Spirit Leads the Journey

Discipleship is not sustained by human strength. It is walked in daily dependence on the Holy Spirit, who empowers, guides, and sustains us each step of the way.

Romans 8:14 says, "Those who are led by the Spirit of God are the children of God." As we continue walking with Jesus, we learn to recognize and respond to the Spirit's leading. We begin praying in the Spirit, living by the Spirit, and bearing the fruit of the Spirit (Galatians 5:22–25). The longer we follow Christ the less we rely on willpower and the more we learn the power of surrender.

This Spirit-led walk is beautifully demonstrated in the life of Barnabas. Though lesser known, he was a vital leader in the early church. Acts 11:24 calls him "a good man, full of the Holy Spirit and faith." Barnabas didn't rely on status or charisma. He walked in quiet obedience, empowered by the Spirit. His faithfulness helped launch Paul into ministry and brought unity to the early church. His journey wasn't marked by spotlight but by Spirit-led service.

There Are Seasons on the Path

Every journey has seasons. Some are marked by growth and momentum, others by waiting and testing.

Before becoming king, David spent years running from Saul. Though anointed, he was hunted. Though chosen, he was chased. His journey continued through caves and valleys. But he didn't abandon the path.

In Psalm 23:4 he writes, "Even though I walk through the darkest valley, I will fear no evil, for you are with me."

The presence of God doesn't always remove the valley, but it sustains us through it. The disciple walks with endurance, trusting that the Shepherd leads every step (Psalm 16:8).

There may be dry seasons when God feels distant. There may be seasons of pruning when He removes what no longer bears fruit (John 15:2). But every season is part of the journey. And every season has purpose.

The Journey Shapes You

Over time the disciple is transformed—not all at once but little by little. The Holy Spirit uses the journey itself to mold us.

Second Corinthians 3:18 says, "We . . . are being transformed into his image with ever-increasing glory." This is not a one-time event. It's a process, a journey. The disciple becomes more like Christ as he or she continues walking with Him.

Timothy, Paul's young protégé, didn't become a leader overnight. He grew under Paul's mentorship, through Scripture, and by enduring hardship. Paul wrote to him, "But you, man of God, flee from all this, and pursue righteousness, godliness, faith, love, endurance and gentleness" (1 Timothy 6:11). Timothy's journey shaped him into a shepherd of churches.

That's what discipleship does, it shapes us for kingdom work. It takes time, pressure, obedience, and the Holy Spirit's fire.

Multiplying the Mission

Discipleship was never meant to stop with us. The journey continues through others when we pour into the next generation of believers. Paul told Timothy in 2 Timothy 2:2, "The things you have heard me say . . . entrust to reliable people who will also be qualified to teach others." This is generational discipleship, passing on what you've received, so that the mission outlives you.

The original disciples didn't just preach the gospel—they raised up leaders, trained new disciples, and sent them out. Paul raised Timothy, Titus, and many others. Peter mentored Mark. Barnabas took John Mark under his wing after Paul rejected him. They weren't just walking for themselves—they were also walking for the kingdom.

If we stop discipling others, the journey becomes self-centered. But when we begin mentoring, teaching, encouraging, and investing in others, we multiply the reach of the gospel. That's what Jesus meant when He said, "Go and make disciples of all nations" (Matthew 28:19). He wasn't just asking us to preach—He was also calling us to reproduce.

Your journey matters not only for your own faith but also for the ones God will entrust to your care. You are called to lead, guide, and raise others up.

When the Journey Feels Hard

Every disciple will eventually walk through a season when the journey feels heavy, when prayers seem unanswered, when progress feels slow, or when obedience feels lonely. Even the strongest believers can grow discouraged, not due to unbelief but because they've walked faithfully for a long time without seeing the fruit they hoped for.

Elijah once reached that point. After calling down fire from heaven and defeating the prophets of Baal, he fled into the wilderness, exhausted and ready to give up. "'I have had enough, Lord,' he said. 'Take my life'" (1 Kings 19:4). But God didn't rebuke him—He refreshed him. God gave him rest, food, and a renewed assignment. He reminded Elijah that the journey wasn't over and that he wasn't alone.

In the same way many who have walked closely with God still find themselves in valleys where strength runs low and hope grows dim. Some of the most faithful disciples in history have hit moments of weariness and wondered if they could keep going. But it's in those moments that the Lord draws near and says, "Get up and eat, for the journey is too much for you" (1 Kings 19:7). He gives us what we need to continue.

Don't mistake fatigue for failure. Don't confuse silence with abandonment. If the road feels hard, it may be because you're walking it faithfully. The enemy resists those who are still on the path. But take heart: God sees you, strengthens you, and walks with you—even in the wilderness.

Faithful in the Silence: John on Patmos

One of the most powerful pictures of a disciple staying faithful in isolation is the apostle John. Long after the early momentum of the church had passed, after most of the other apostles had been martyred, John found himself exiled to a barren island called Patmos.

He was not there on vacation. Revelation 1:9 tells us, "I, John . . . was on the island of Patmos because of the word of God and the testimony of Jesus." He was punished for preaching the gospel and left alone, without a congregation, without support, and without visible fruit. It would have been easy to feel forgotten.

But John didn't give up. He worshiped. He listened. And there, in that quiet and lonely place, God gave him one of the most powerful revelations in all of Scripture. The disciple who once rested on Jesus's chest at the Last Supper became the prophet who saw the Lamb on the throne, the Alpha and Omega, the returning King.

Sometimes our most faithful seasons come when no one sees. Sometimes the clearest visions are born from the quietest moments. John endured, and his obedience became a blessing to every generation after him.

You may not always feel fruitful. You may not always feel seen. But when you remain faithful in the silence, God still speaks. He still moves. And He still uses you.

The Finish Line Is Ahead

Discipleship doesn't stop with this life. It carries us forward into eternity.

Paul wrote in 2 Timothy 4:7–8, "I have fought the good fight, I have finished the race, I have kept the faith. Now there is in store for me the crown of righteousness." These words weren't just the reflections of a tired man—they were the declaration of someone who had endured pain, prison, rejection, and hardship, yet never gave up. Paul kept walking, kept believing, and now his reward was waiting.

That is our hope too—that we would finish well, holding fast to our faith all the way to the end.

Not everyone who starts the journey finishes it. Some turn back. Some grow cold. True disciples press on, not by strength alone but through the sustaining grace of Christ. They endure, grow, and stay in step with the Spirit, even when the road is long.

This is the call of discipleship: to keep walking with Jesus, to keep growing in Him, to stay the course regardless of what comes.

Your journey isn't just for a season—it's for a lifetime, step by step, day by day, until that final moment when you stand before Him and hear the words, "Well done, good and faithful servant."

Reflection

What phase of the journey am I in today?
Am I bearing fruit? Am I helping others walk this path?
Who around me is watching my walk and learning from my example?
How can I become a Paul or Peter for someone else in his or her walk?

Prayer

Jesus, thank you that the journey doesn't end, it deepens. Thank you for walking with me every step. Give me strength to keep going, to keep bearing fruit, and to keep sharing your love. Help me to disciple others, to be faithful in season and out, and to walk as you walked. I want to finish strong and raise others up along the way. In Jesus's precious name. Amen.

Chapter 15

Finishing Well

There's something sacred about finishing your journey. It's not about being perfect, it's about being faithful. The call to discipleship is not just about how we start or even how we grow—but about how we finish.

The Christian life is a race, and every lap matters. But the final lap, when we look back at what we've poured out for Christ, matters deeply. It is the legacy we leave, the impact we've made, and the final testimony we offer to the world.

Finishing well is about more than surviving life's storms—it's about being refined through them and pointing others to Jesus all the way to the end.

Fighting the Good Fight

As noted earlier, Paul's journey was full of trial, shipwreck, beatings, imprisonments, and betrayal, but he finished with his eyes fixed on Jesus. He knew the value of endurance and the beauty of arriving in God's presence still clinging to faith.

He didn't say he had done it all perfectly. He said he had kept the faith. And for a disciple, that's finishing well.

Jesus—the Perfect Finisher

Jesus didn't come just to live—He came to finish.

On the cross with His final breath He declared, "It is finished" (John 19:30). It wasn't a whisper of surrender; it was a cry of victory. The mission was complete. The plan of redemption was fulfilled. The debt of sin was paid in full.

He said in John 17:4, "I have brought you glory on earth by finishing the work you gave me to do." Jesus was faithful to the very end, through betrayal, mockery, beatings, and the weight of the world's sin.

He didn't turn back. He didn't fall short. He crossed the finish line, carrying our salvation with Him. He is the one we follow, the author and the finisher of our faith. And because He finished, we can too.

Faithful to the End

Jesus said in Revelation 2:10, "Be faithful, even to the point of death, and I will give you life as your victor's crown."

This is the call of every disciple: to remain faithful to Jesus, even when it costs us everything. For many in the early church, finishing well meant giving their lives. For others, like John, it meant enduring exile, isolation, and silence. But no matter the path, they reached the end still declaring that Jesus is Lord.

Whether our journey is long or short, public or private, easy or painful, the calling remains the same: be faithful to the very end.

We look at the life of Peter, once afraid, now bold unto death. We see Paul, once a persecutor, now a tireless apostle. We remember John, once a simple fisherman, now the final apostolic voice, writing truth even from exile.

Their lives echo through time, not because they were loud but because they were loyal.

Redemption after Failure

Some finish strong, not because they never fell but because they got back up.

Peter denied Jesus three times on the darkest night of his life. But Jesus met him in grace, not judgment. With love and purpose, He restored Peter's calling: "Feed my sheep." And Peter did. He rose again in boldness and helped lead the early church with courage.

Samson also stumbled, not in fear but in compromise. He traded his strength for pleasure and pride. Yet in his final moment, blinded and broken, he cried out to God. And God heard him. His last act brought down the enemy's temple and delivered victory for Israel (Judges 16:28–30).

Then there's David. He failed in sin, fell in shame, and nearly lost everything. But he returned in repentance. He humbled himself, turned back to the Lord, and was still called a man after God's own heart.

The journey to the finish line isn't always clean. Sometimes it's marked with scars. But the grace of God is deeper than every failure and stronger than every fall. Finishing well doesn't require perfection. It requires getting up again and again and trusting the one who lifts us back up.

Leaving a Legacy

Each disciple left something lasting:

Peter left the early church strengthened and rooted in grace.

Paul left a theology of salvation and mission that changed the world.

John left letters of love and a heavenly vision of hope.

Thomas left faith planted across Asia.

Timothy, Mark, Silas, and Barnabas all lived and died as second-generation torchbearers.

And so will you. The lives you've discipled, the children you've loved, the community you've served—these are your legacy.

Finishing well means leaving behind something that will outlive you, people who walk stronger with Jesus because of your faith.

Generational Discipleship

You weren't called just to believe—you were called also to lead others into belief.

Discipleship doesn't end with you. A mature disciple becomes a teacher, a spiritual parent, and a living example. Just as Paul poured into Timothy, and Jesus into the Twelve, we are called to pass on what we've received.

This is the heart of generational discipleship: a faith that multiplies.

A life well lived isn't one that ends in isolation but is one that raises up others to run their race. Your legacy begins when your obedience inspires someone else's.

Biblical Finishers

The Bible is filled with examples of men who finished well. Some did it through bold leadership. Others endured in quiet obedience. What they shared was faithfulness—not perfection but perseverance.

Moses: Faithful in the Wilderness

Moses is a reminder that finishing well doesn't mean finishing flawlessly. Though he disobeyed God at Meribah and was not permitted to enter the promised land (Numbers 20:12), God still called him faithful.

Moses led through wilderness, rebellion, and weariness. He interceded for the people, endured their complaints, and walked closely with God. Deuteronomy 34:10 says, "Since then, no prophet has risen in Israel like Moses, whom the Lord knew face to face."

He finished well, not because he crossed into Canaan but because he never walked away from God's presence.

Caleb: Still Asking for Mountains

At eighty-five years of age Caleb said, "I am still as strong today as the day Moses sent me out. . . .. Now give me this hill country" (Joshua 14:10–12). Caleb never stopped believing in God's promises. He was still ready to fight, still trusting in the Lord's strength.

Finishing well doesn't mean slowing down in your faith. It means continuing to take spiritual ground, even in the later seasons of life.

Caleb teaches us that there's no spiritual retirement, only deeper surrender and greater trust.

Joshua: Leading Others to Finish

Joshua's final words still echo through time: "But as for me and my household, we will serve the Lord" (Joshua 24:15).

He didn't just lead Israel into the promised land—he also led them to renew their commitment to God, a covenant that would shape future generations.

His strength was proved not only in battle. It was also revealed in his boldness to stand firm when the culture around him drifted. His life reminds us that spiritual leadership doesn't fade with age; it grows deeper with time.

Daniel: Finishing in the Shadows

Daniel remained faithful under Babylonian and Persian kings, living most of his life in exile. He prayed daily, fasted humbly, and heard from God in dreams and visions.

He never led a physical army. He never held a pulpit. But he influenced kings and remained a man of integrity until the end.

Finishing well doesn't always look public. Sometimes it looks like decades of faithfulness behind closed doors and a heart that never bows to idols.

Simeon: A Life of Waiting

Simeon was a righteous man who had waited his entire life for the Messiah. The Holy Spirit had revealed to him that he would not die before seeing the Lord's Anointed (Luke 2:25–26). And he believed.

When Mary and Joseph brought Jesus into the temple, Simeon took the child in his arms and declared, "Sovereign Lord, as you have promised, you may now dismiss your servant in peace" (Luke 2:29).

Simeon's whole life was long obedience in the same direction. He didn't finish with a grand ministry or a visible legacy—he finished with a fulfilled promise and a heart of worship.

Some disciples finish their race not on the battlefield but in the quiet assurance that they waited well.

Modern-Day Examples

Across the world today there are men and women finishing well in quiet faithfulness.

A rural pastor preaching for decades with no spotlight but eternal impact

A grandmother praying for generations and raising a lineage of faith

A missionary serving unknown to the world but known deeply by God

A father discipling his children after work with weary hands and a willing heart

They may not be written into history books, but their names are known in heaven. These are the finishers. These are the faithful. These are the ones who will hear, "Well done."

Eternal Glory

There's a reason we keep going.

James 1:12 says, "Blessed is the one who perseveres under trial because, having stood the test, that person will receive the crown of life that the Lord has promised to those who love him."

Hebrews 12:1–2 reminds us to "run with perseverance the race marked out for us, fixing our eyes on Jesus, the pioneer and perfecter of faith."

And Peter adds, "You will receive the crown of glory that will never fade away" (1 Peter 5:4).

These aren't metaphors. They are promises from God to those who finish well.

The race we run has a finish line, and waiting at that finish line is the Savior we love. He will wipe away every tear. There will be no more death or mourning or pain (Revelation 21:4) — just the joy of being home.

We don't run for applause. We run for the King. And when we cross that line, every trial will have been worth it.

The Master's Words

Every disciple longs to hear one day the words spoken by Jesus in Matthew 25:21: "Well done, good and faithful servant!"

Not "Well known"
Not "Well liked"
But "Well done"

These are the words that await every soul who has walked the long road of discipleship with sincerity and surrender. The crown of life is not for the strongest—it's for the faithful.

Final Charge

You've walked far. You've sacrificed much. You've chosen obedience when it was hard. You've grown in the Spirit, and you've borne fruit.

And now as you keep walking toward the finish line, know this: you are not alone. Jesus is with you. The Spirit is within you. The Father is waiting for you.

Others are watching your journey—younger believers, seekers, future disciples. Let them see Jesus in your endurance. Let them be inspired by your faith.

So don't stop now.

The same Spirit who called you will carry you. The same Jesus who forgave you will sustain you. And the same Father who chose you is waiting with open arms.

Finish strong. Speak truth. Love deeply. Walk humbly. Pour into the next generation. Raise up disciples who will keep running long after you're gone.

There is no greater honor than to lay down your life in full surrender and hear those words echo through eternity: *"Well done, good and faithful servant."*

Reflection

Am I running this race with eternity in view?

What will my spiritual legacy be?

Who am I investing in so that the mission continues beyond me?

Prayer

Father, I want to finish well—not in pride, not in comfort, but in faithful obedience to you. Let my life be a testimony to your grace. Help me raise others up to walk this same road. I surrender every breath to you. May my final words and final steps honor the name of Jesus. Amen.

Final Blessing

Disciple of Jesus—you are not forgotten. You are not finished. You are chosen. You are filled with the Holy Spirit. And you are sent to live a life that glorifies Christ.

Run your race. Keep the faith. Finish well.

And one day may the heavens ring with the words *"Well done, my good and faithful servant!"*

📖 Scripture Mention List

Chapter 1: Author's Testimony

None

Chapter 2: The Invitation

None

Chapter 3: Growing in Faith

John 14:26; Proverbs 3:5–6; James 1:22

Chapter 4: A Growing Call to Serve

None

Chapter 5: Called to Represent Christ

Matthew 4, Luke 4; Acts 9; 1 Corinthians 12

Chapter 6: The Call to Follow Fully

Matthew 4; Luke 4; John 15

Chapter 7: Becoming like the Master

Luke 2:46–52; Luke 2:52; Luke 4; Luke 15; John 8:12; Matthew 28:19; Luke 14:28; Luke 5:16

Chapter 8: Walking in His Footsteps

John 15; John 13; Acts 10

Chapter 9: Living as a Disciple

Acts 2; Acts 9; Acts 4:13; John 15; Acts 10; Luke 22; John 4; Luke 8; John 13

Chapter 10: Making Disciples

John 4; Acts 9; Acts 9:27; Acts 10; Acts 20; Acts 4; Acts 4:12; Acts 5; Acts 4:13; Acts 1

Chapter 11: The Spirit-Led Life

Luke 10; John 20; Luke 22:42; Acts 9; Acts 18:26; Matthew 9:37–38; Philippians 1:6

Chapter 12: Enduring in the Walk

Acts 7; Genesis 37–50; Luke 1–2; Acts 9; Acts 15:36–40; Acts 1–28; Revelation 1

Chapter 13: Perseverance

Acts 2; Acts 5; Acts 7; Revelation 1:9; Matthew 4; Hebrews 12:1–2; Genesis 37–50; Luke 23; Luke 22:61–62

Chapter 14: The Journey Continues

Mark 3:17; 2 John 1:6; Revelation 1; John 13:23; John 15:2; Matthew 4:19; John 21:19

Chapter 15: Finishing Well

John 21; Matthew 28:19; 1 Kings 19:4–7; John 15:2; 2 Timothy 4:7; 2 Timothy 2:2

Full Scripture Index

Chapter 1: Author's Testimony

Romans 8:28

Chapter 2: The Invitation

Ephesians 2:8-9; Romans 10:9-10; Luke 23:42-43; 2 Corinthians 5:17; John 10:10; James 1:17; Hebrews 11:6; Matthew 11:28; Galatians 6:10; Galatians 6:9-10

Chapter 3: Growing in Faith

Romans 12:2; Galatians 5:16-17; Proverbs 3:5-6; Colossians 3:1-3; 2 Timothy 3:16-17; James 1:22; Philippians 1:6; James 1:2-3

Chapter 4: A Growing Call to Serve

Matthew 4:19; 1 John 2:3-6; Joshua 24:15; Matthew 25:35-40; Matthew 20:26-28; Galatians 6:10; 1 Peter 4:10; John 12:26

Chapter 5: Called to Represent Christ

2 Corinthians 5:20; Matthew 5:16; 1 John 2:3-6; Philippians 2:15; Acts 1:8; Galatians 5:22-23; Romans 10:14-15; 1 John 1:9; Colossians 3:23-24; 1 Timothy 1:15-16; 2 Timothy 3:12; Galatians 6:9; Matthew 9:9

Chapter 6: The Call to Follow Fully

Luke 9:23; Luke 2:49; Luke 2:52; Mark 10:21; Luke 14:28; Philippians 3:8; John 15:16; Matthew 28:20; Matthew 28:19; John 8:12; Luke 22:42; Luke 5:16

Chapter 7: Becoming like the Master

1 John 2:6; Luke 2:49; Romans 8:29; John 14:26; John 13:7; Galatians 5:22-23; Ephesians 5:1-2; Matthew 20:25-28; John 13:14-15; Philippians 2:5-8; Luke 15:7; Mark 1:35

Chapter 8: Walking in His Footsteps

1 Peter 2:21; 2 Timothy 3:16–17; Psalm 119:105; Luke 5:16; Matthew 26:39; Psalm 139:1–3; Psalm 139:23–24; Colossians 2:6–7; 2 Corinthians 5:17; Philippians 2:5; John 5:19; Luke 9:23; 2 Corinthians 5:7; John 1:7; Psalm 23:4; John 15:5; Romans 12:1–2

Chapter 9: Living as a Disciple

1 John 2:6; John 15:4; Galatians 5:22–23; John 13:35; 1 Corinthians 13:2; Matthew 5:16; Luke 9:23; 2 Timothy 2:3; Acts 5:41; Galatians 6:9; Romans 1:16; Acts 4:12; John 1:14; Matthew 28:19; 1 Thessalonians 2:8; Proverbs 9:9; Galatians 2:20

Chapter 10: Making Disciples

Matthew 28:19–20; Acts 1:8; John 1:4;, 1 Corinthians 11:1; 2 Timothy 2:2; Matthew 4:19–20; Philippians 4:9; Acts 18:26; Luke 8:2; Luke 8:3; Luke 14:27; Acts 7; Matthew 9:37–38

Chapter 11: The Spirit-Led Life

Galatians 5:25; Luke 2:49; Matthew 4:1; Luke 1:38; Luke 8:2; Luke 7:1–10; John 4:46–54; Acts 2; Acts 8; Acts 7; Romans 8:14; Romans 8:11; Galatians 5:16; Galatians 5:22; Romans 8:5; 1 Corinthians 2:12

Chapter 12: Enduring in the Walk

Galatians 6:9; John 21:17; James 1:2–3; 2 Corinthians 11:23–27; Romans 5:3–4; Hebrews 12:1–2; Philippians 3:14; Luke 5:16; Luke 22:44; Hebrews 12:2; 2 Timothy 4:7; Hebrews 6:10

Chapter 13: Perseverance

James 1:12; Luke 8:15; John 16:33; Romans 5:3–4; Hebrews 10:36; Luke 22:61–62; John 20:19; John 21; Matthew 4:1–11; Luke 22:44; Hebrews 12:2; Romans 12:12; 2 Corinthians 11:24–27; 2 Timothy 4:7; Hebrews 6:10; Galatians 6:9

Chapter 14: The Journey Continues

Colossians 2:6; Philippians 3:12; Philippians 1:6; Matthew 7:13–14; Acts 5:29; Romans 8:14; Galatians 5:22–25; Acts 11:24; Psalm 23:4;

Psalm 16:8; John 15:2; 2 Corinthians 3:18; 1 Timothy 6:11; 2 Timothy 2:2; Matthew 28:19; 1 Kings 19:4; 1 Kings 19:7; Revelation 1:9; 2 Timothy 4:7–8

Chapter 15: Finishing Well

2 Timothy 4:7–8; John 19:30; John 17:4; Revelation 2:10; Judges 16:28–30; Numbers 20:12; Deuteronomy 34:10; Joshua 14:10–12; Joshua 24:15; Luke 2:25–29; James 1:12; Hebrews 12:1–2; 1 Peter 5:4; Revelation 21:4; Matthew 25:21

Postscript: From My Heart to Yours

If you've made it this far, thank you. Thank you for walking this journey—not just through these pages but also toward the heart of God.

I didn't write this book because I have it all figured out. I wrote it because I've lived it—the failures and the breakthroughs, the surrender and the struggle, the joy and the cost. And through it all I found this one truth unshakable: Jesus is worth it.

Discipleship is not a title, it's a life. It's not always easy, but it's always holy—because He walks with you. So, keep walking. Don't turn back. Don't settle for simply belief when you were made for obedience. Don't stop at growth when you were called to multiply.

Follow Jesus. Finish well. And as you do, may your life bring glory to the one who called you.

By His grace,
—Mac McKee (Cornelius Martin McKee)

❦ Acknowledgments and How to Grow Further

First and always—to my Savior, Jesus Christ. You rescued me. You changed me. You called me.

To the Holy Spirit, who convicts, teaches, and strengthens.
To God the Father, who never gave up on me—even when I gave up on myself.

To my family, my brothers and sisters in Christ, and to every other soul who's ever spoken a word of encouragement into my life—thank you.

To you, the reader — keep going. Find a Bible-believing church. Immerse yourself in God's Word. Pray every day. Surround yourself with faithful believers. Find a mentor. And when God calls you—become one.

Let this book be a beginning, not an end. Let it fuel your journey forward into deeper discipleship, greater fruitfulness, and a life that points others to Jesus.

To God be the glory—forever and ever. Amen.

NOTES

www.ingramcontent.com/pod-product-compliance
Lightning Source LLC
Chambersburg PA
CBHW050912160426
43194CB00011B/2381